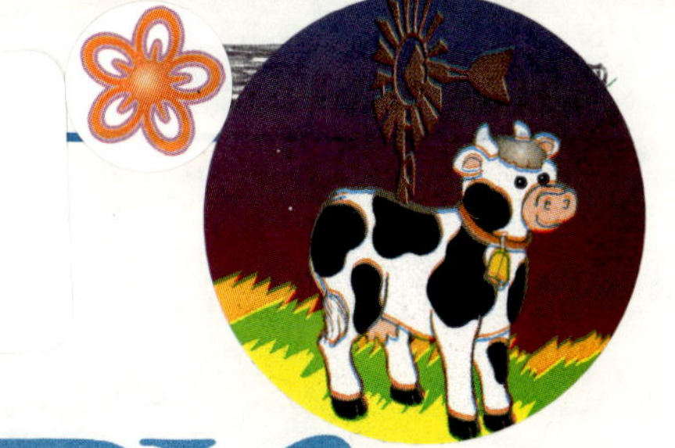

PATCHWORK PATTERNS

from Bible Stories

Judy Rehmel

Augsburg Fortress • Minneapolis

CONTENTS

CREDITS
Cover Design: Eric Lecy
Illustrator: Suzanne M. Pohle

PATCHWORK PATTERNS FROM BIBLE STORIES
Twelve Designs for Quilts and Crafts

International Standard Book No. 0-8066-2520-1

INTRODUCTION

Quilting is said to have begun in China and was done for centuries in ancient Egypt. Marco Polo brought the art to Europe after seeing the practical quilted clothing of the Chinese. In Europe, quilted clothing was used under the heavy metal armor of the knights, and ladies wore quilted petticoats to ward off the icy winter cold. European quilting was done on whole cloth. Two large pieces of fabric were laid out with a layer of wool between them, and the designs were created with elaborate quilting motifs.

When Europeans arrived in North America in the 1600s, there were no mills producing textiles. Fabrics were imported from England. And some settlers raised sheep for wool, spun the wool into yarn, and wove their own fabric at home. Fabrics of all types were so precious that frugal homemakers began to create quilts by sewing their small scrap pieces together to create a piece large enough for a quilt. Thus arose the distinctively American craft, the pieced quilt.

Gradually, quilting became more a matter of art and less a matter of necessity. It also became more of a social event. Several women might each contribute a block to a quilt. The blocks were then sewn together, and the group would have a quilting bee to finish the quilt. Sometimes each quilter would embroider her name on the blocks she had contributed.

Church women throughout the United States have created thousands of quilts for shipment overseas. These quilts may be used as everything from blankets to walls in a small, crowded home. While most of these quilts are utilitarian by design, their creation has helped keep the art of quilting alive.

The first American quilts were crazy quilts in which any size or shape piece was used just as it was. The desire for order and beauty probably led to such simple patterns as the Four-square and the Nine-patch. As quilt designs developed, probably every known geometric shape has come to be used in thousands of configurations and variations.

Eventually quilt patterns began to acquire names, which reflected the lives of the people who made them. A name might include a happening of the day, a geographical location, a physical object, a political figure, or a Bible story.

This book contains a collection of 12 patterns named for Bible stories. Some date from before the Revolutionary War. Others are from the twentieth century. All of the patterns have been prepared for 12-inch blocks. These designs can be combined to create a full-size quilt. Or, one pattern, such as the butterfly, can be used for all the blocks in a quilt, with each butterfly done in a different color.

Biblical references and notes are included with each pattern. I hope you have as much enjoyment creating your quilting project as I have had putting this book together.

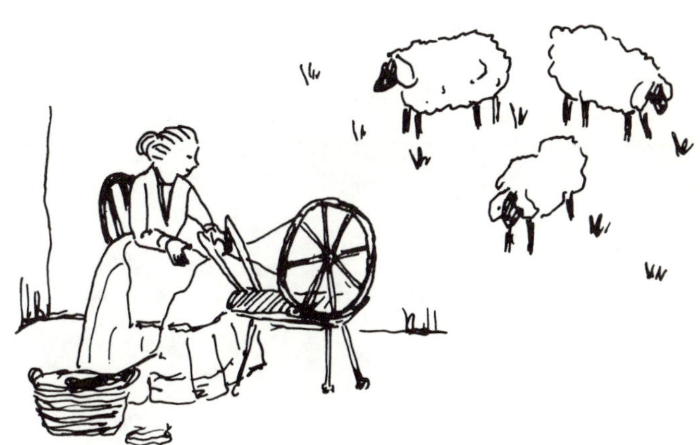

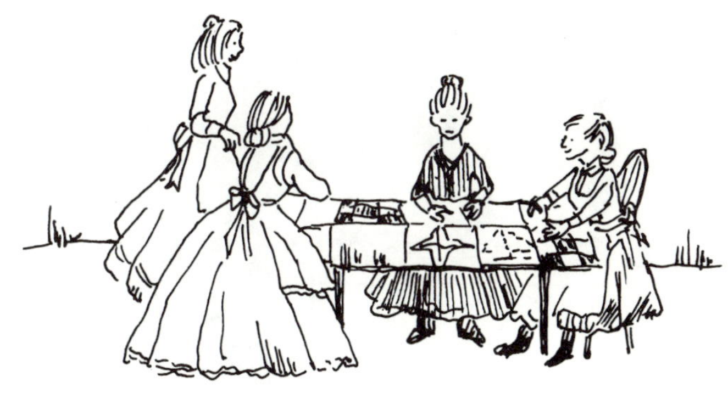

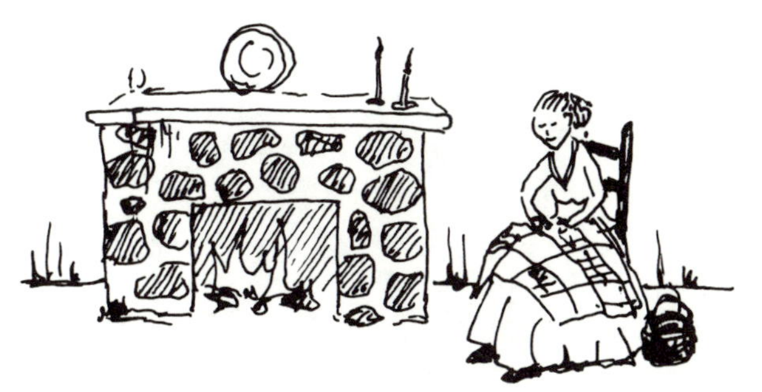

INSTRUCTIONS

1. Carefully plan your quilting project, whether you will be making a full-size quilt or one of the crafts suggested for each pattern.
2. Select colors that are pleasing to you and that complement one another well. If necessary, consult an art book and study the recommended combinations of primary and secondary colors.
3. Fabrics of the same fabric type are recommended. Print and solid fabrics of 100% cotton or of a cotton/polyester blend are both good materials. Some quilters do not like to use the two different types of fabric for aesthetic reasons. Others are concerned that different fabrics will shrink at different rates or in different directions, but there is usually no problem if all fabric is washed before starting the project.
4. Pre-wash and machine dry all fabrics to be used, washing lights and darks separately. This will ensure that all shrinkage is out of the fabric. Press all fabric before marking and cutting.
5. Each pattern piece is marked with a suggested grain line. You may wish to alter this to accommodate a particular fabric pattern. Make a test block to get a better idea of how a block will look. A test block also gives you a chance to check the fit of the pieces and to make sure a pattern is within your abilities.
6. Cutting patterns out of freezer paper, very fine grain sandpaper, or see-thru plastic may make cutting the fabric easier and more accurate.
7. Be sure to cut accurately. A seam allowance of ¼-inch is marked by the dashed line. The solid line is the cutting line.
8. Pieces may be sewn together by hand or by machine. It is best not to cross seam lines when stitching. Corners and points will be more precise. Seam allowances should be pressed in one direction, not pressed open.
9. To complete most of the projects, put together the top layer, use a layer of cotton or polyester batting, and add a plain or patterned backing. Quilting can be done in an appropriate design or by following the lines of the individual pieces.
10. Depending upon the project, the edges will need to be finished. A bias binding in matching or contrasting colors may be neatly attached.

PALM LEAF

Alternative Names
Hosanna, Palm Leaves, Hosannah!

Variations
This pattern is usually made in dark green and white. Variations include making each leaf from a different fabric; dividing the corner square into two triangles; or doing alternate sections with white leaves on a dark background.

Bible Verse: John 12:13
They took palm branches and went out to meet him, shouting, "Hosanna!"
"Blessed is he who comes in the name of the Lord!"
"Blessed is the King of Israel!"

Pattern Notes
The reference to the crowds waving palm branches when Jesus entered Jerusalem is the most familiar one from the Bible, although palms are mentioned frequently. The palm is a very useful tree. Date palms produce dates for eating. The fibers of some palm trunks may be twisted into ropes or woven into mats. The seeds of some palms provide food for camels. The sap can be fermented into wine. And the trunk is cut into lumber and the leaves woven into many useful objects. This very old quilt pattern probably originated in Maine before the Revolutionary War.

Pieces Needed for Each Block
A—4 light solid
B—4 dark green print, 4 dark green print reversed
C—4 light solid, 4 light solid reversed
D—4 dark green print, 4 dark green print reversed
E—4 light solid, 4 light solid reversed
F—4 dark green print, 4 dark green print reversed
G—4 light solid, 4 light solid reversed

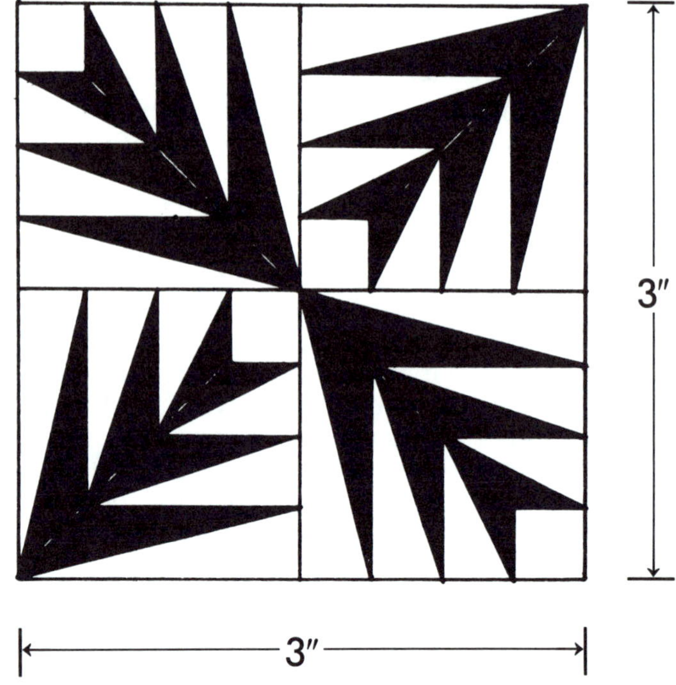

Suggested Order of Assembly

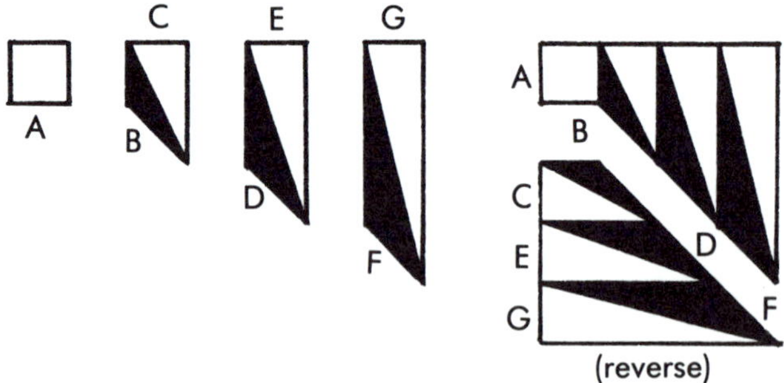

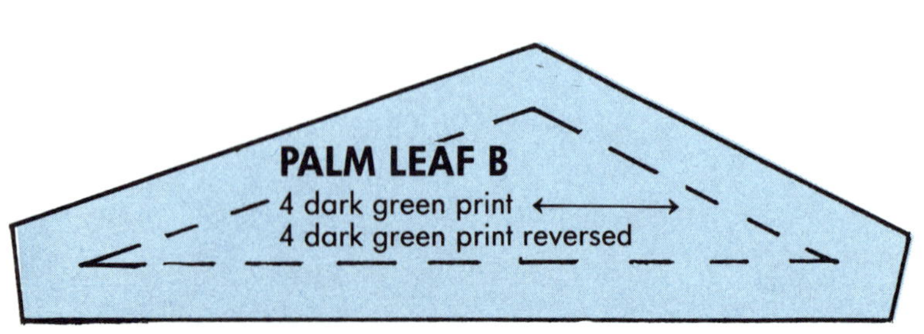

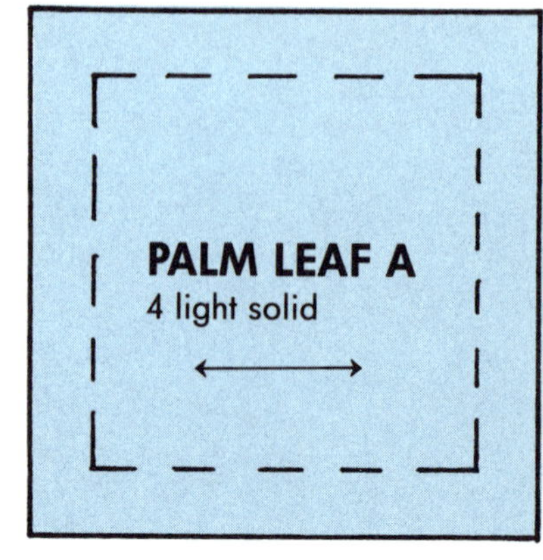

Alternative Project

Combine quilting and banner making skills by using the Palm Leaf pattern with the word "Hosanna!" for a Palm Sunday banner.

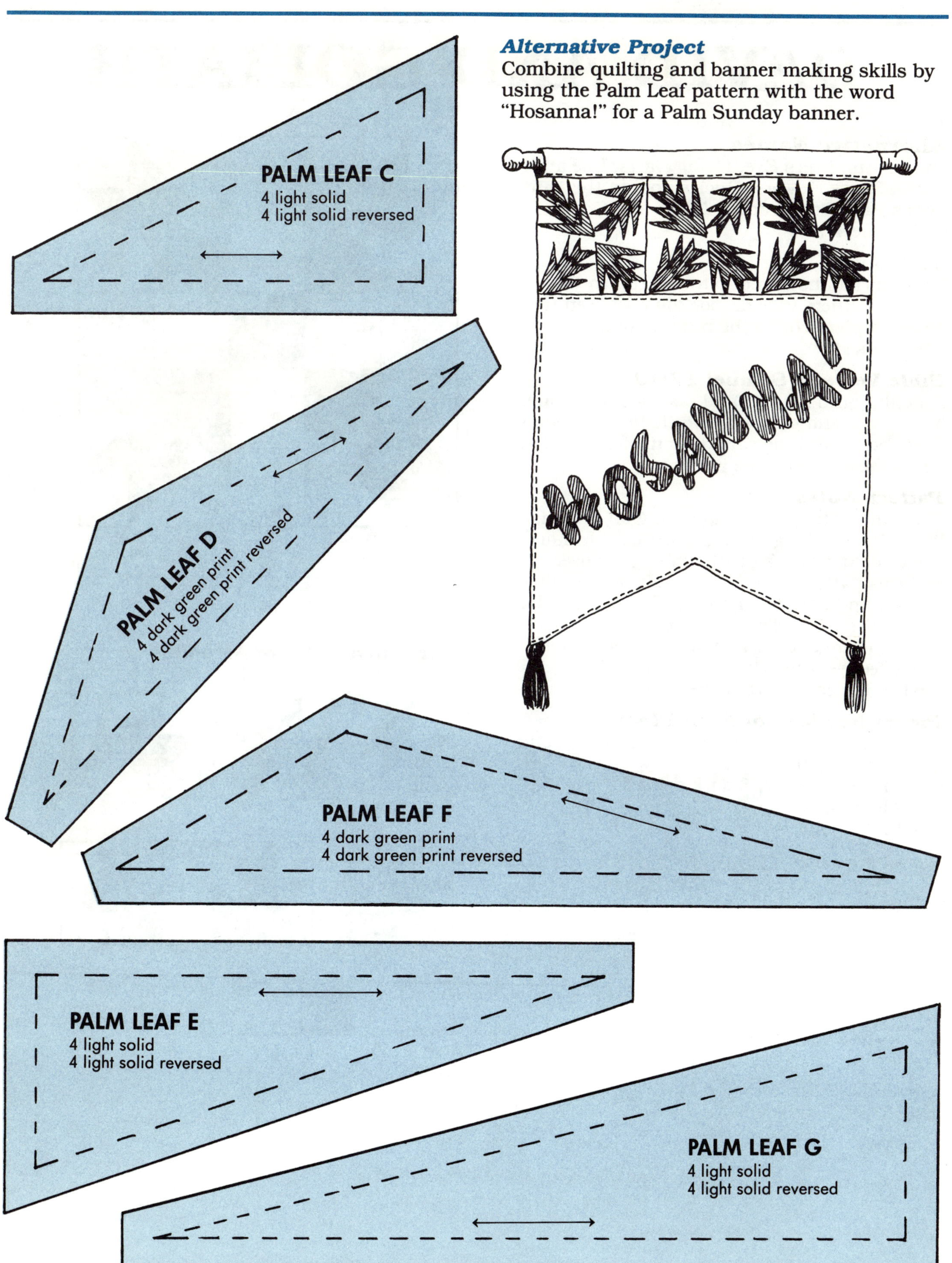

DAVID AND GOLIATH

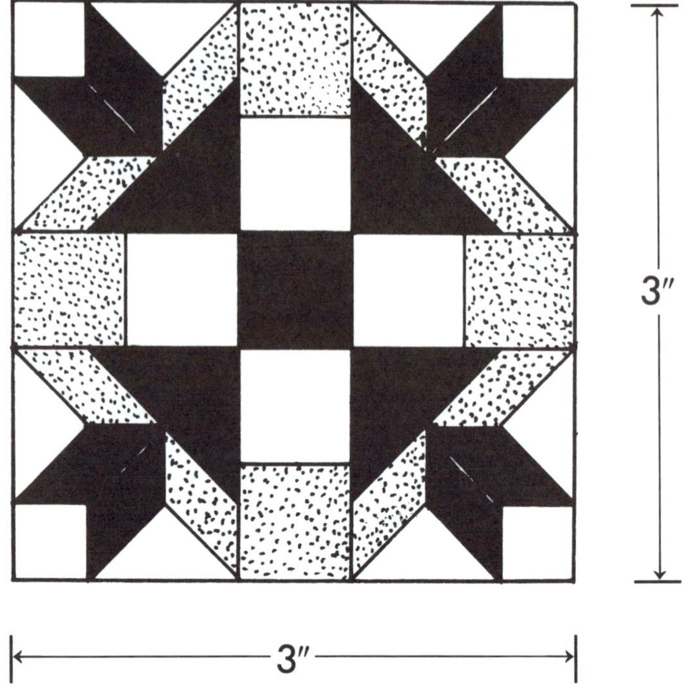

Alternative Names
Four Darts, Bull's Eye, Flying Darts, Doe and Darts, Fancy Flowers, Duck's Foot in the Mud, Bear's Paw, Duck Paddle, Cross and Crown, and Goose Tracks

Variations
Some variations do not have "darts" in the corners. Others vary proportions between the different pieces or in the number of different fabrics used.

Bible Verse: 1 Samuel 17:49
Reaching into his bag and taking out a stone, he slung it and struck the Philistine on the forehead. The stone sank into his forehead, and he fell facedown on the ground.

Pattern Notes
The story of the boy David taking on the huge Philistine has long been a favorite Bible story used to illustrate the truimph of good over evil, and this pattern traditionally has been quilted in light and dark fabrics only. But using a dark print with a complementary plain fabric of medium intensity against a light background is very effective also. This pattern goes back at least to the early part of the twentieth century.

Pieces Needed For Each Block
A—1 dark print, 4 light solid, 4 medium solid
B—4 dark print
C—8 medium solid, 8 dark print
D—8 light solid
E—4 light solid

Suggested Order of Assembly

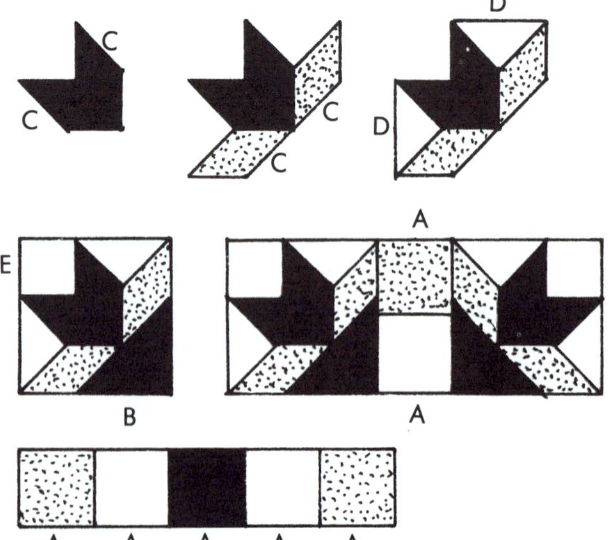

Alternative Project

Pot holders for an attractive buffet table perk up church dinners.

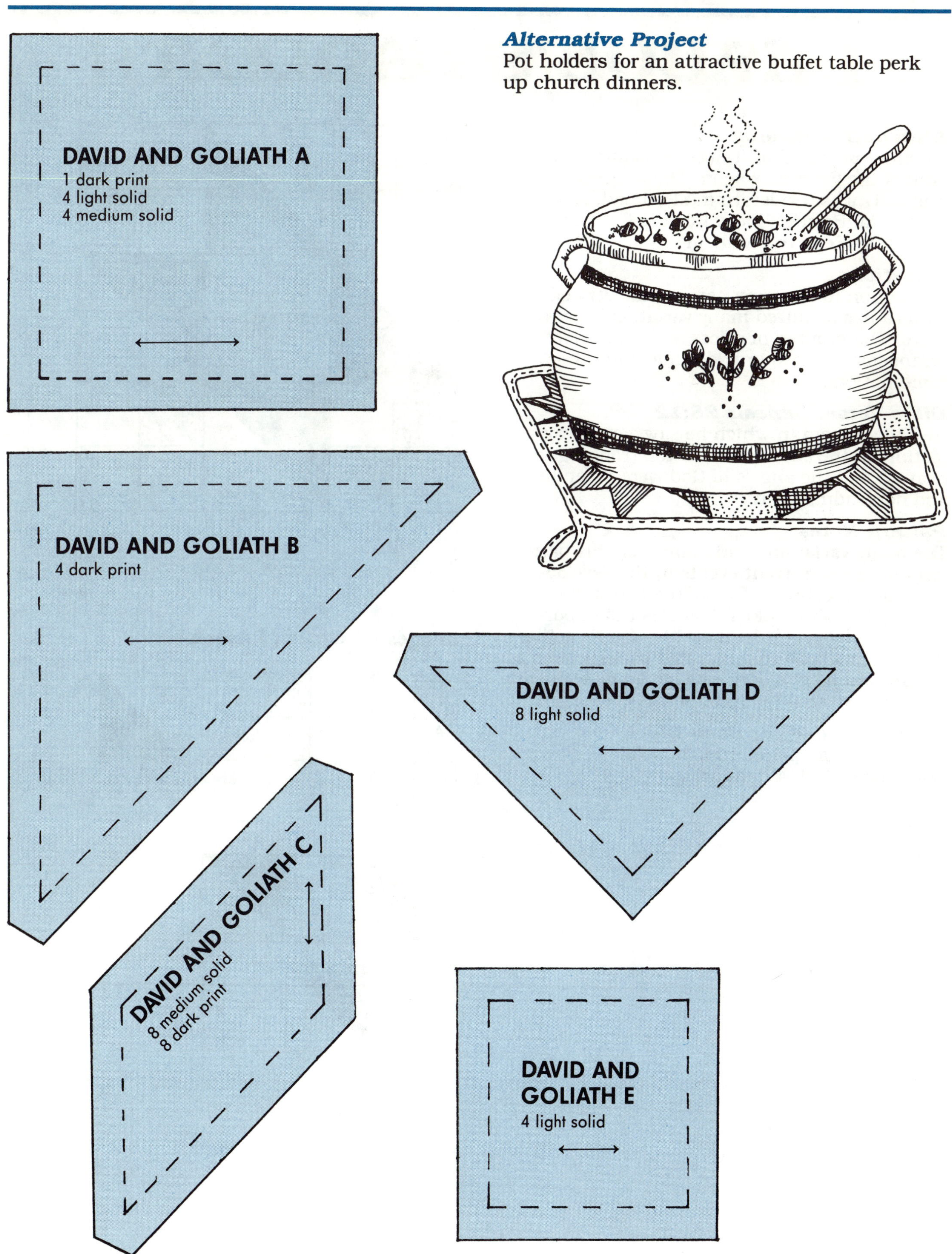

JACOB'S LADDER

Alternative Names
Stepping Stones, The Tail of Benjamin's Kite, Trail of the Covered Wagon, The Railroad, Wagon Tracks, Underground Railroad, Road to California, Bowtie, Rocky Road to California, and Rocky Road to Oklahoma

Variations
In addition to its many names, this very old pattern has acquired many variations over the years. The number of colors and the variety of arrangements used provide almost limitless combinations.

Bible Verse: Genesis 28:12
He had a dream in which he saw a stairway resting on the earth, with its top reaching to heaven, and the angels of God were ascending and descending on it.

Pattern Notes
The many variations and names for this pattern tend to reflect current events in the development of our country. One of the oldest of the names, "Jacob's Ladder," reflects the importance of religion in the daily life of early settlers. When set without sashing, this pattern gives a distant feeling of a very long ladder or stairway, the stairway seen by Jacob in his dream.

Pieces Needed for Each Block
A—10 medium print, 10 light solid
B—4 dark solid, 4 light solid

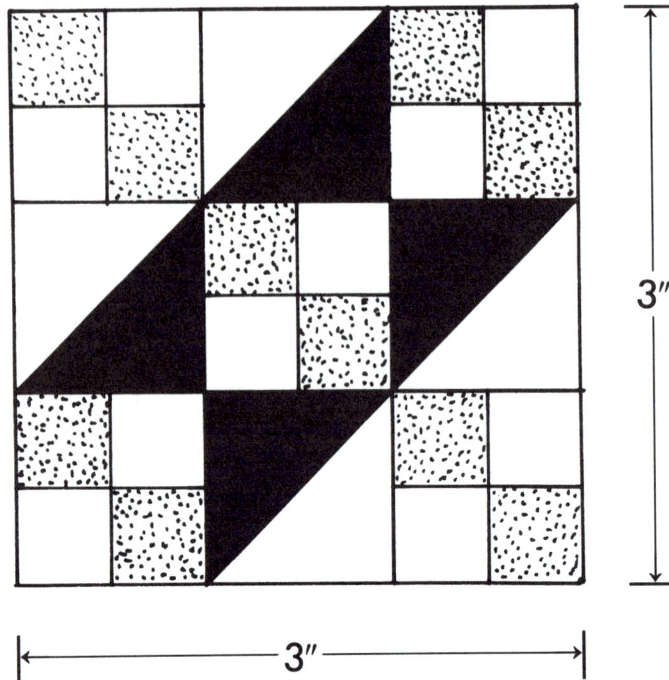

Suggested Order of Assembly

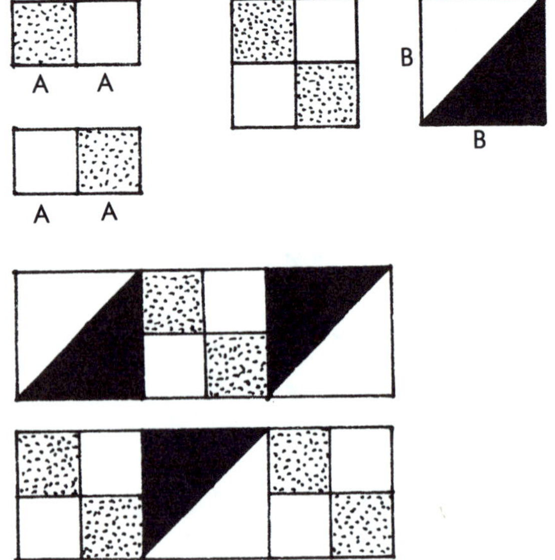

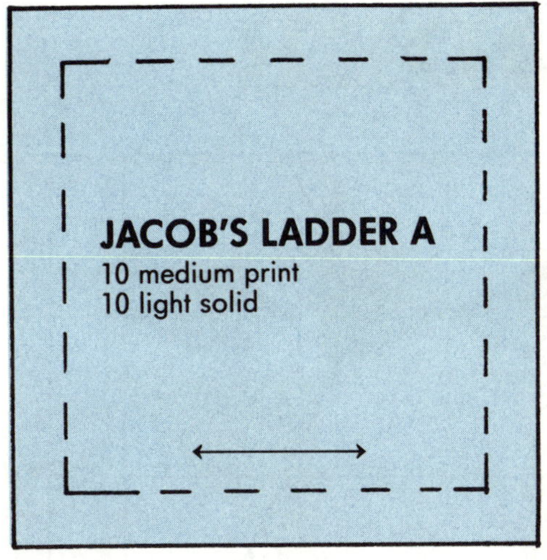

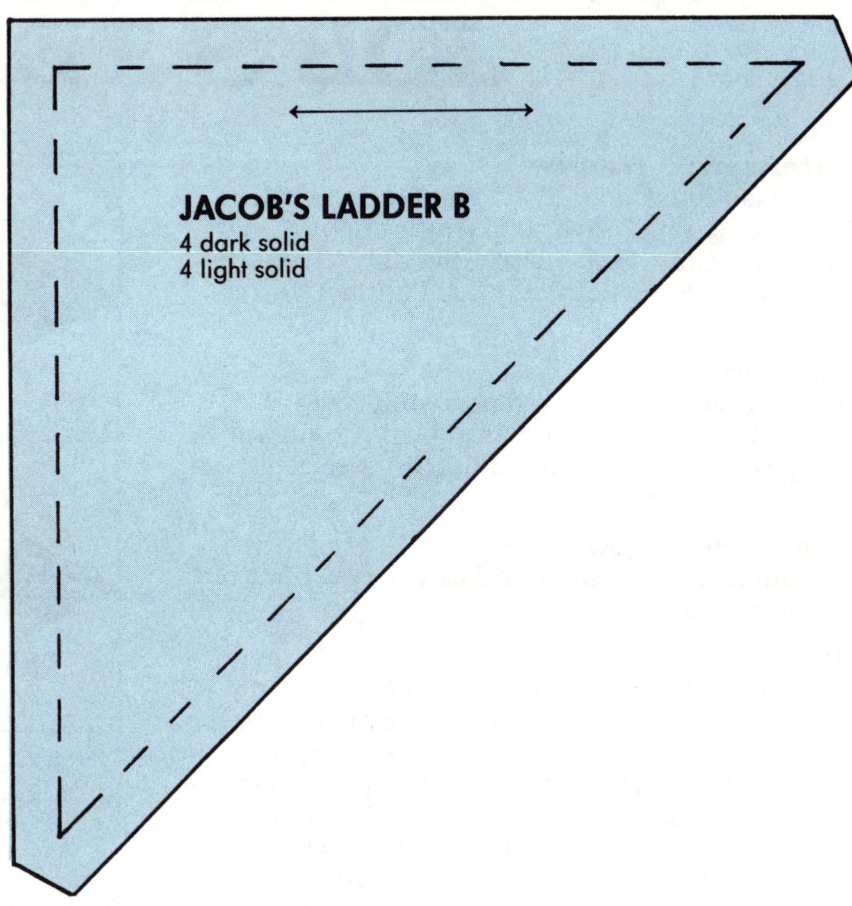

Alternative Project

Although this pattern would be effective in many projects, a full-size quilt is very attractive.

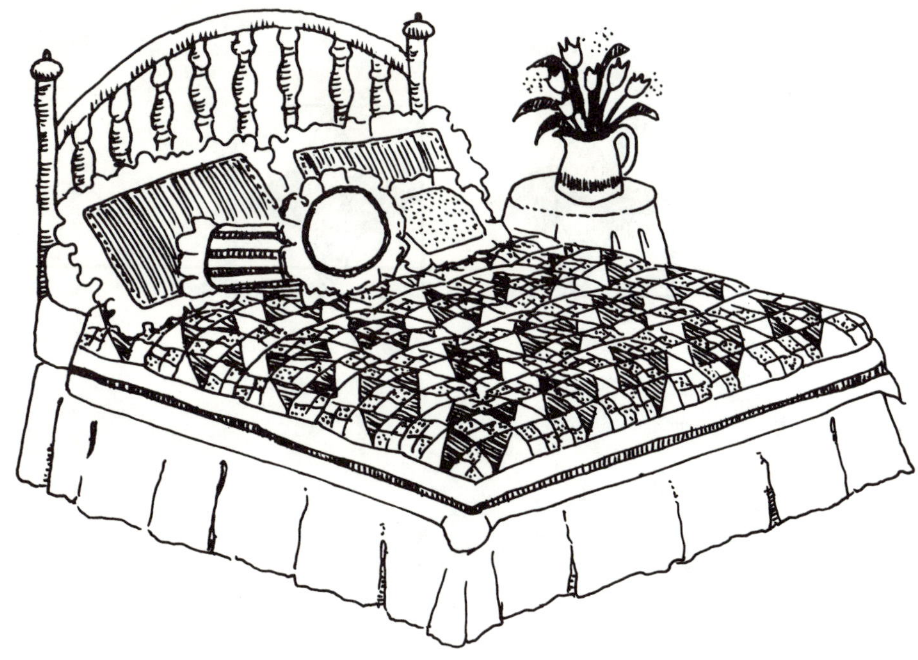

JOB'S TEARS

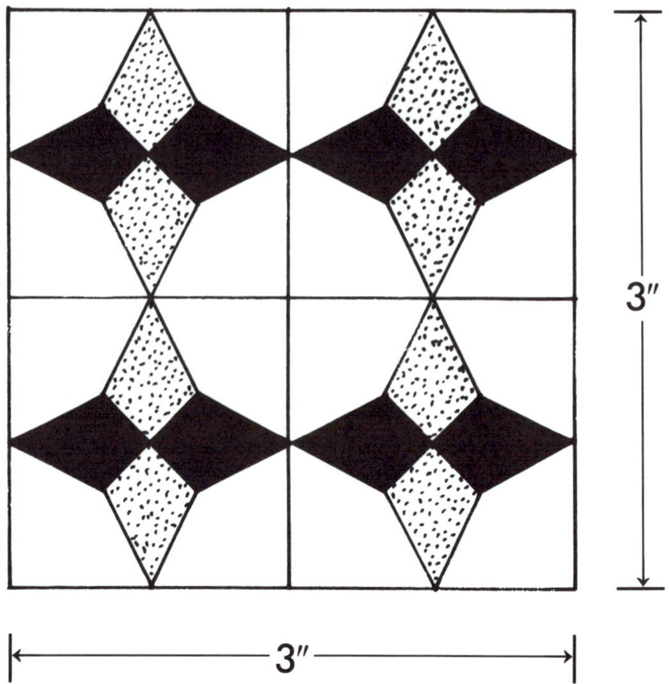

Alternative Names
Arkansas Snowflake, Four Points, Snowball, The Kite Quilt, Periwinkle, Hummingbird, Arkansas Star, Four-point Kite, Job's Trouble, Snowflake, Four-pointed Star, Pontiac Star, Star Kites

Variations
This pattern can be used as a single star instead of the four stars as shown. Changing the position of the solid and print pieces gives a great variety of effects.

Bible Verse: Job 16:20
My intercessor is my friend as my eyes pour out tears to God.

Pattern Notes
One book of the Bible is devoted to Job, a man who was tested numerous times by God. The pattern used here makes a good scrap quilt with each tear in a different pattern or color. The use of many colors attests to the many trials of Job. Another pattern with the same name, "Job's Tears," has four oval shapes similar to an old variety of bean plant cultivated in flower gardens.

Pieces Needed for Each Block
A—8 dark solid, 8 medium print
B—16 light solid

Suggested Order of Assembly

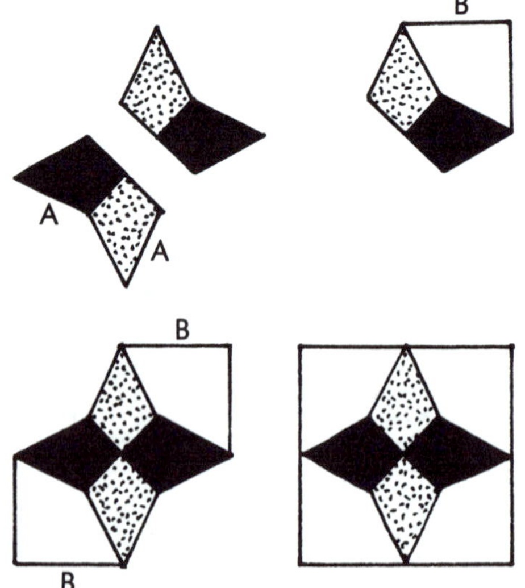

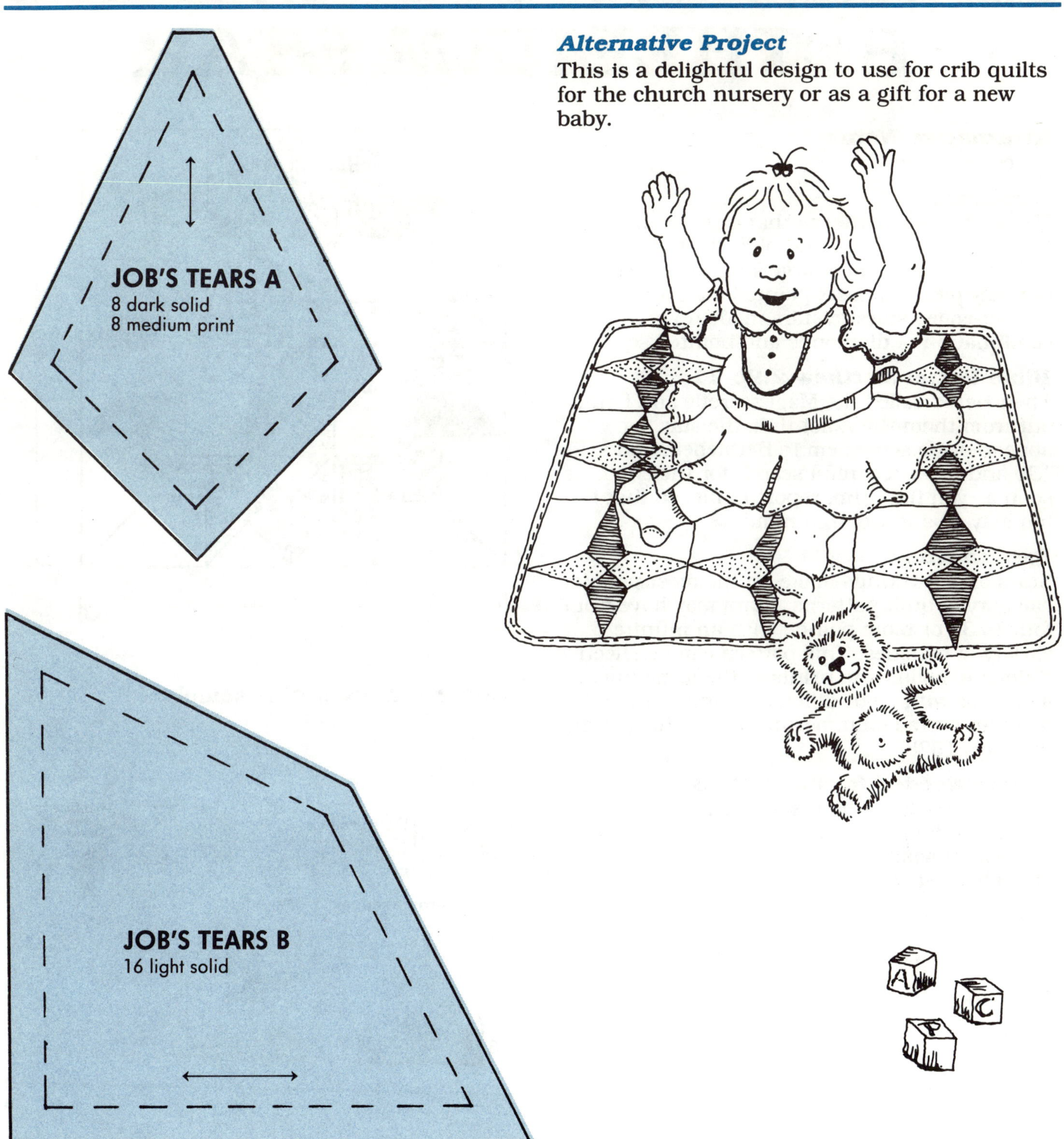

Alternative Project

This is a delightful design to use for crib quilts for the church nursery or as a gift for a new baby.

BETHLEHEM STAR

Alternative Name
Dutch Rose

Variations
There are many patterns that bear the name "Bethlehem Star" or "Star of Bethlehem." These patterns range from a large single star made up of many pieces to a six-pointed star, and feather-edged stars to stars made up of a combination of diamonds and pointed squares.

Bible Verse: Matthew 2:9b-11
Then Herod called the Magi secretly and found out from them the exact time the star had appeared. He sent them to Bethlehem and said, "Go and make a careful search for the child. As soon as you find him, report to me, so that I too may go and worship him."

Pattern Notes
Stars of many kinds make up the most popular category of quilt patterns. Stars may have from four to 32 or more points, with an infinite variety of twinkles. This pattern can be effective if done in solids and prints of the same hue; all solids; or with eight different prints, which gives an overall shimmering effect. This pattern predates 1928.

Pieces Needed for Each Block
A—4 light solid, 4 light solid reversed
B—32 as desired
C—8 light solid
D—8 light solid

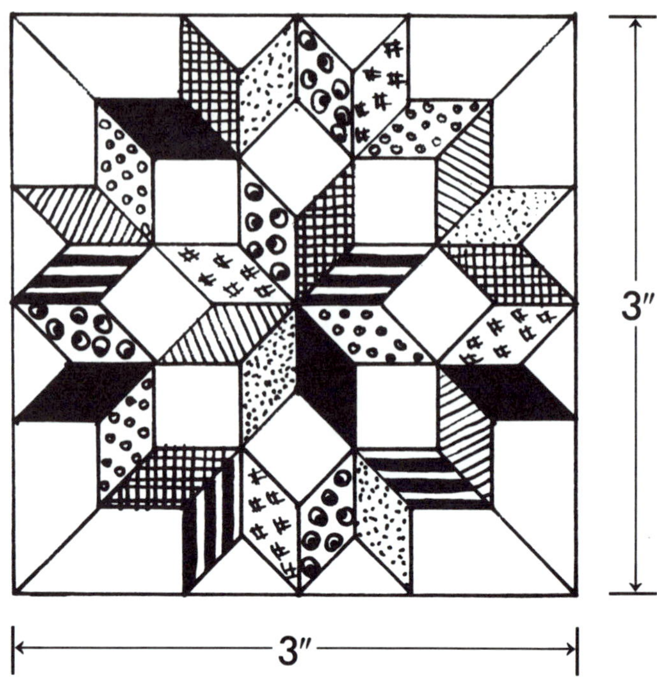

Suggested Order of Assembly

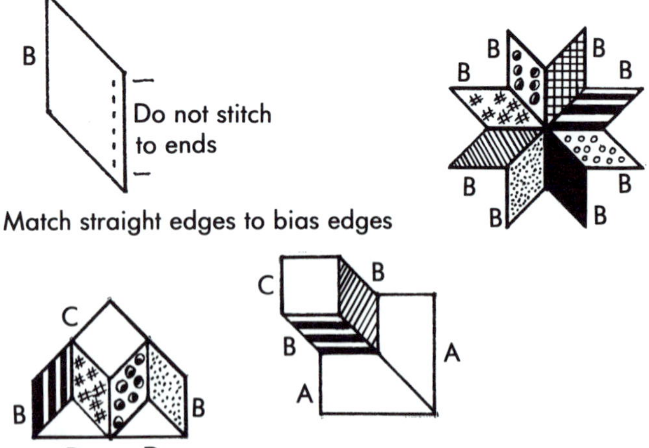

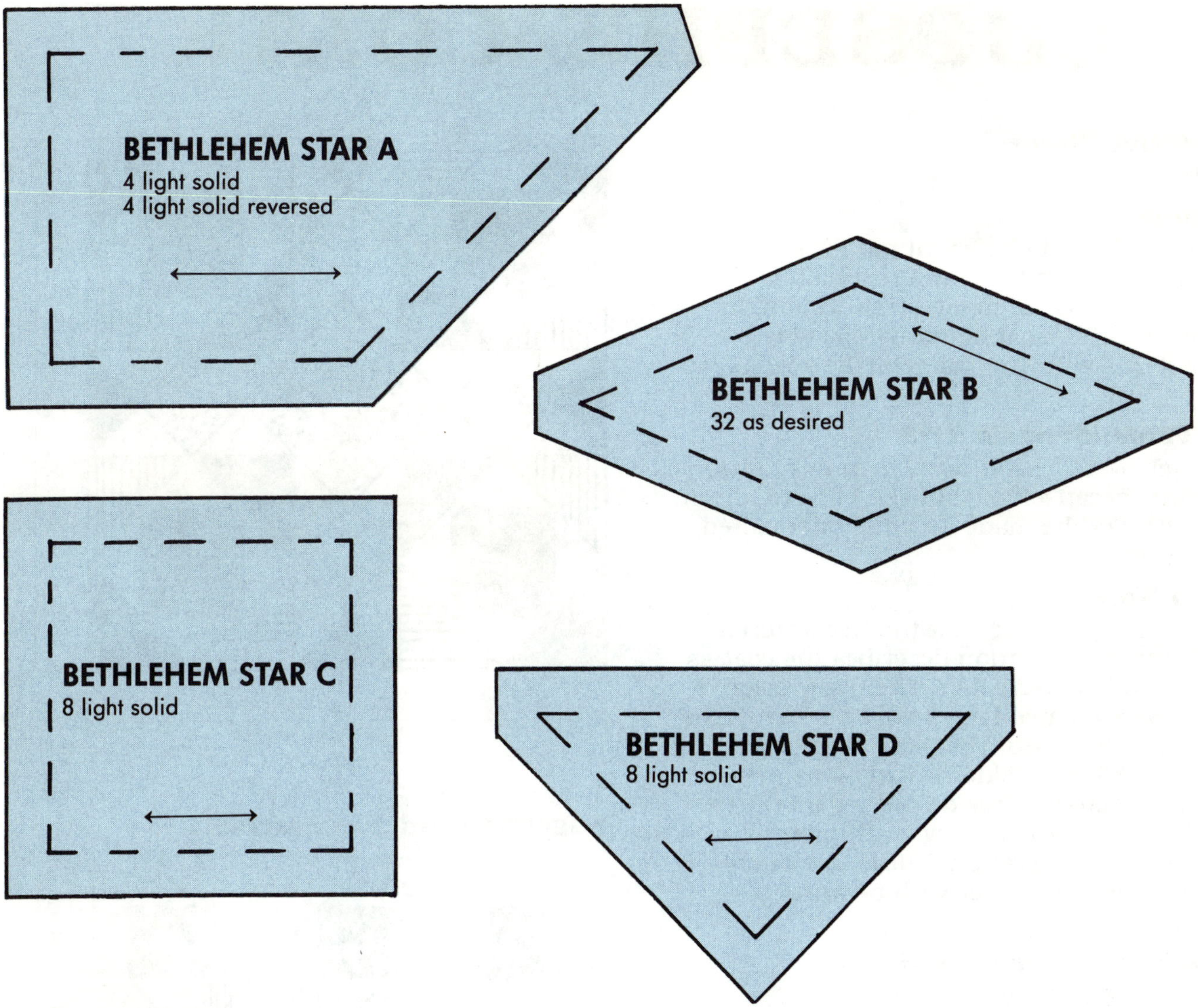

BETHLEHEM STAR A
4 light solid
4 light solid reversed

BETHLEHEM STAR B
32 as desired

BETHLEHEM STAR C
8 light solid

BETHLEHEM STAR D
8 light solid

Alternative Projects

Paraments may be done in blue for the Advent season.

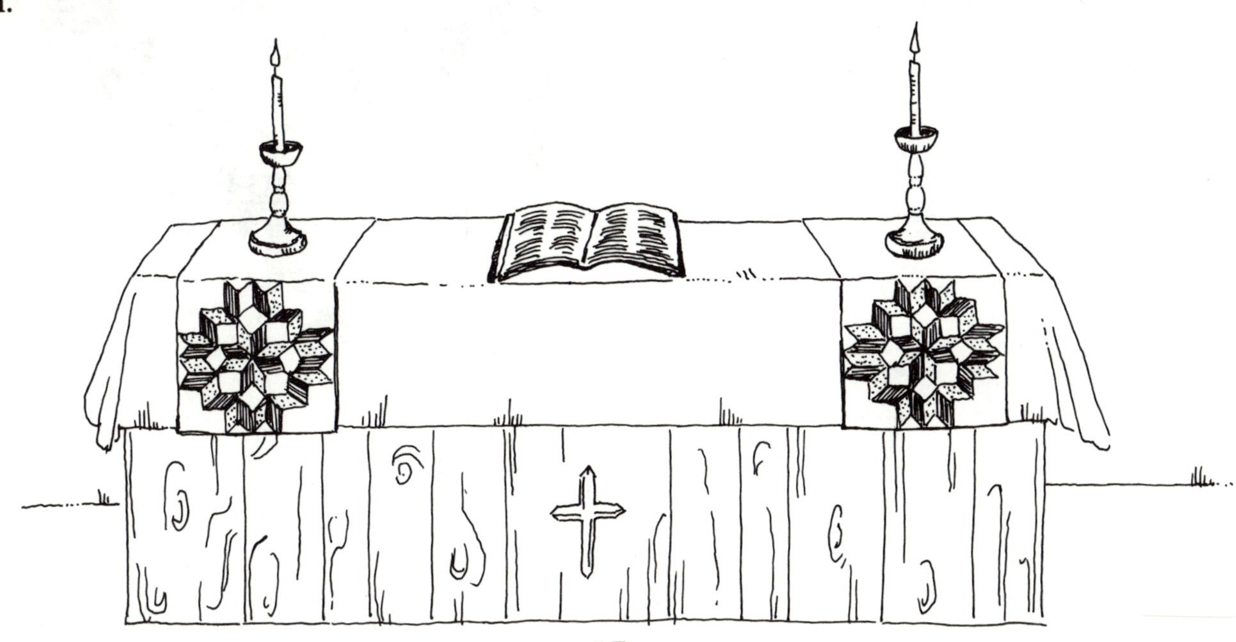

JOSEPH'S COAT

Alternative Name
Scrap Bag

Variations
There are at least 11 different patterns that use this name. The one thing that they all have in common is the use of many bright colors. In keeping with the "coat of many colors" reference, patterns with this name make good scrap quilts.

Bible Verse: Genesis 37:3
Now Israel loved Joseph more than any of his other sons, because he had been born to him in his old age; and he made a richly ornamented robe for him.

Pattern Notes
It is interesting to note that the New International Version translation describes the coat as a "richly ornamented robe." The many-colored patterns were created long before modern translations were done. But the "coat of many colors," described in older translations, has inspired artisans as they helped tell a favorite Bible story about the man who ultimately saved his people from starvation. These blocks are attractive when set either with or without sashing.

Pieces Needed for Each Block
A—8 dark solid, 8 medium solid
B—8 dark solid, 32 light solid
C—4 dark solid
D—1 light solid matching hue
E—4 light solid matching hue

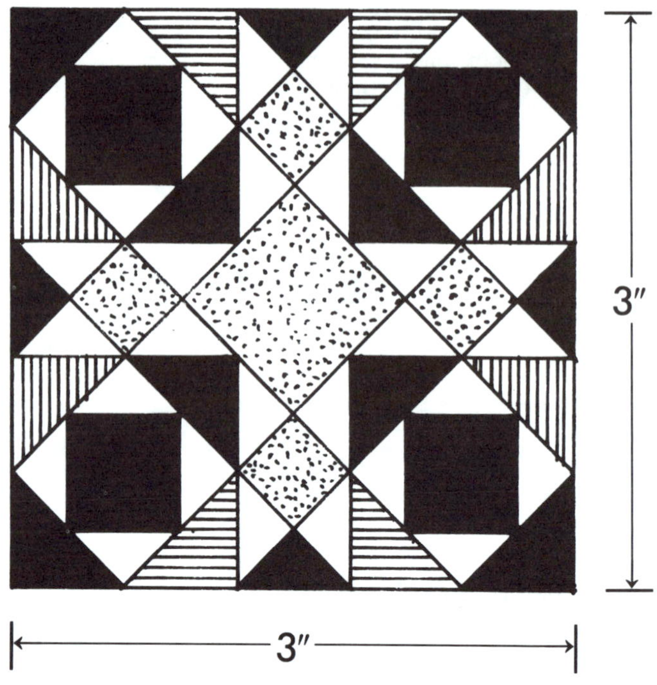

Suggested Order of Assembly

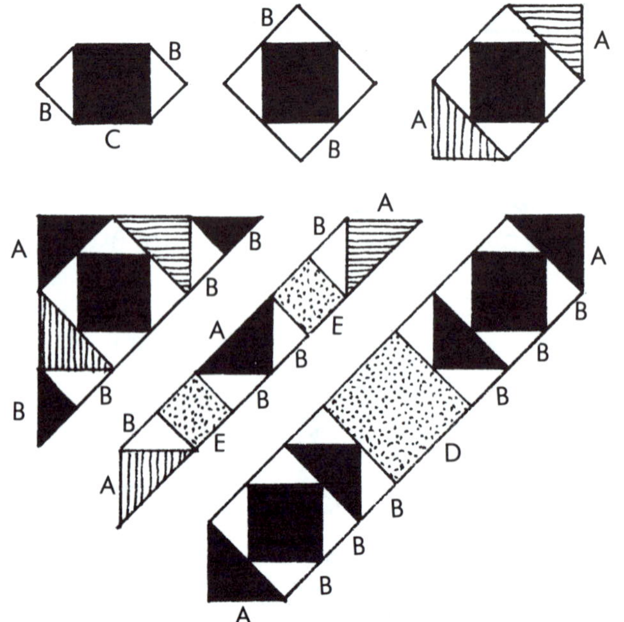

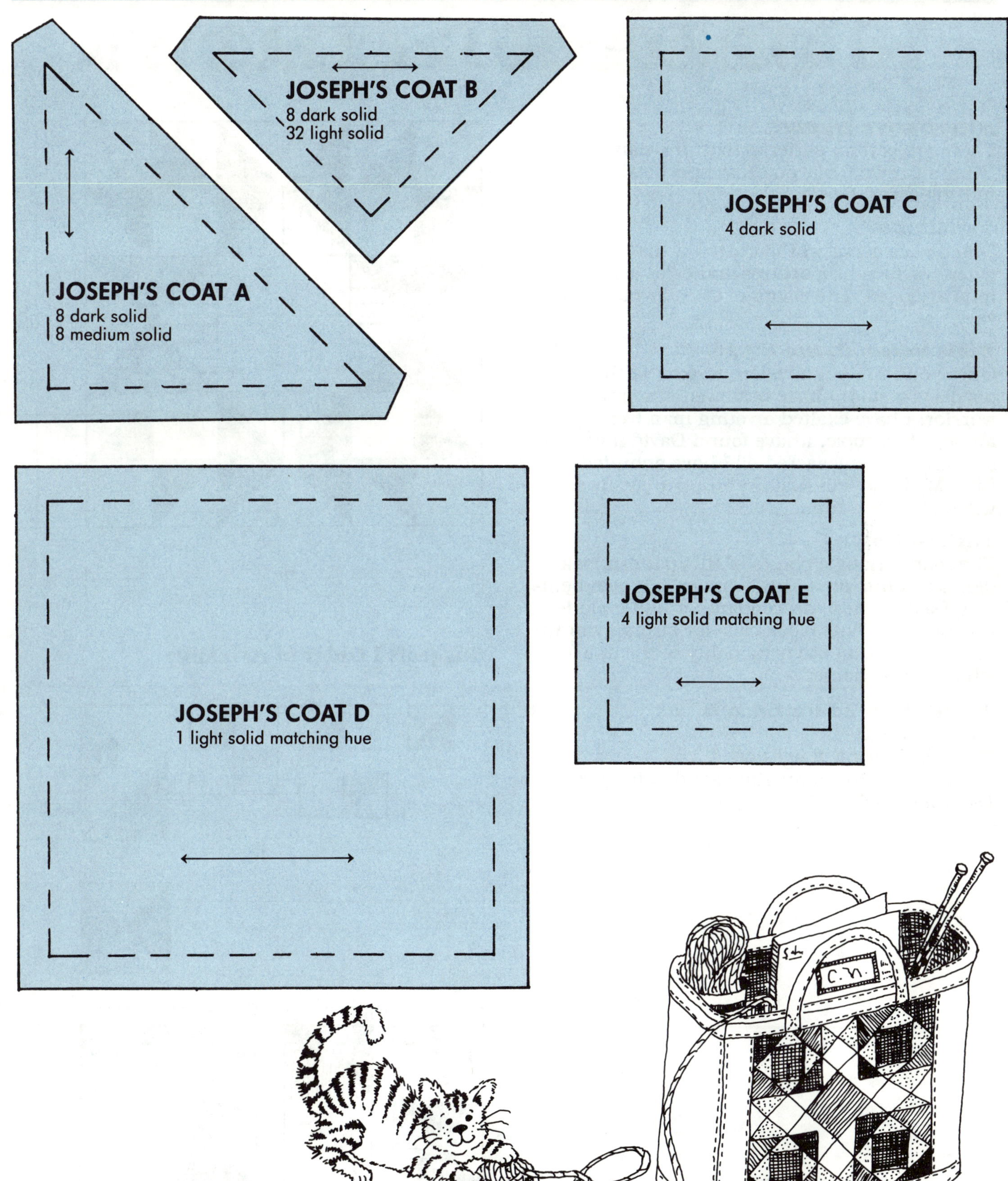

Alternative Project

This pattern would be a good choice for a bright tote bag.

KING DAVID'S CROWN

Alternative Names
There are several patterns with the name "King's Crown," but no other specifically refers to King David.

Variations
Differences occur in the center of the block, where various proportions and color combinatons are used. The colors of the star points may vary.

Bible Verse: Psalm 89:19-21
Once you spoke in a vision, to your faithful people you said: I have bestowed strength on a warrior; I have exalted a young man from among the people. I have found David my servant; with my sacred oil I have anointed him. My hand will sustain him; surely my arm will strengthen him.

Pattern Notes
The many triangle points of this pattern look like the points on a king's crown, a crown befitting David, whose descendants would include the Messiah. This block calls for strong, vibrant colors, reflecting the personality of the one for whom it was named.

Pieces Needed for Each Block
A—8 light solid
B—8 dark print, 8 light solid
C—8 dark print, 4 medium solid, 4 light solid
D—1 light solid

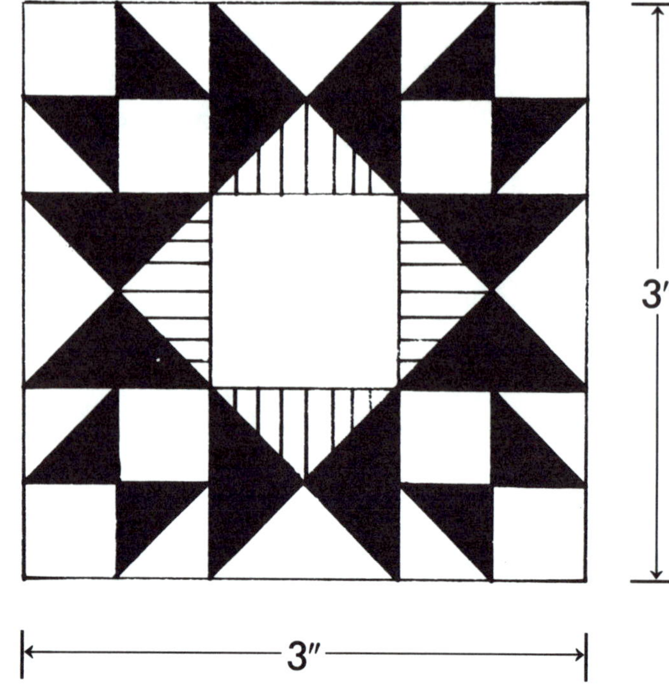

Suggested Order of Assembly

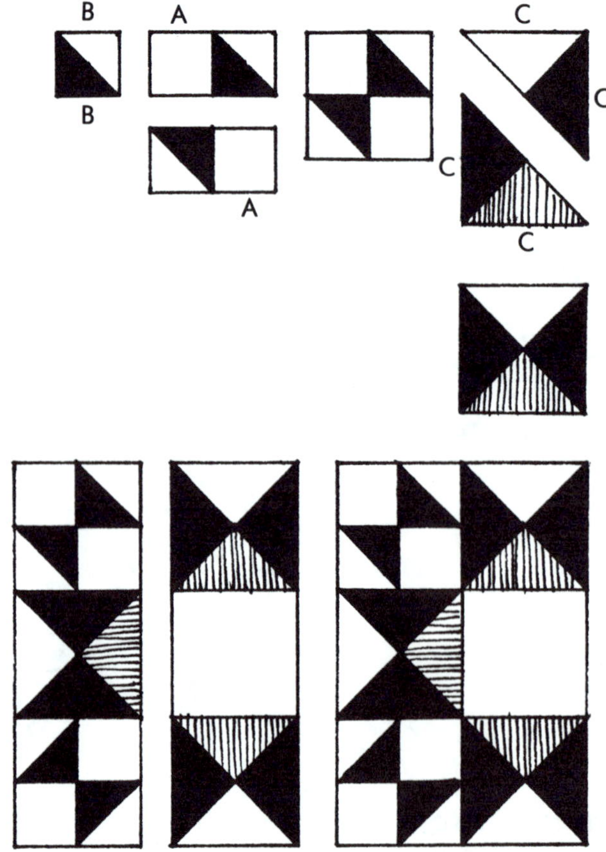

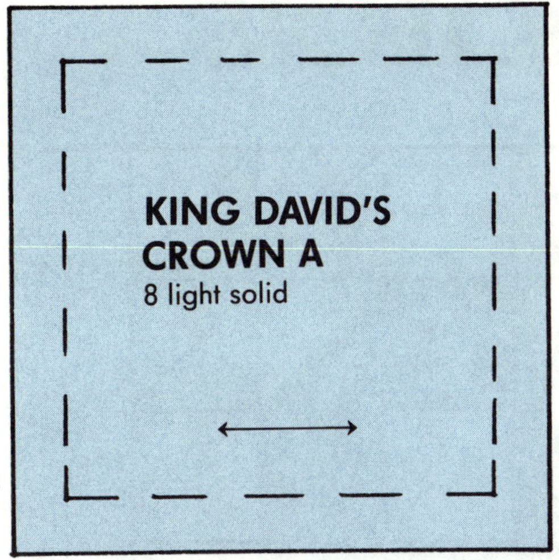

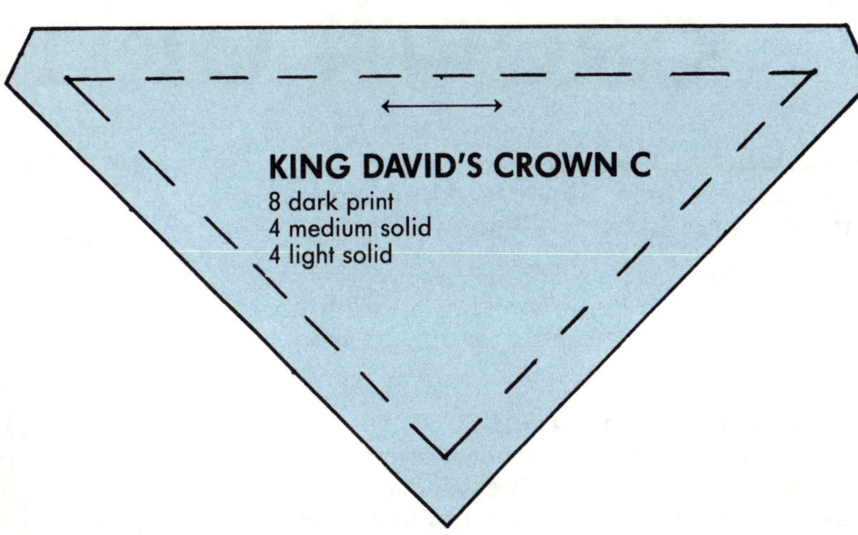

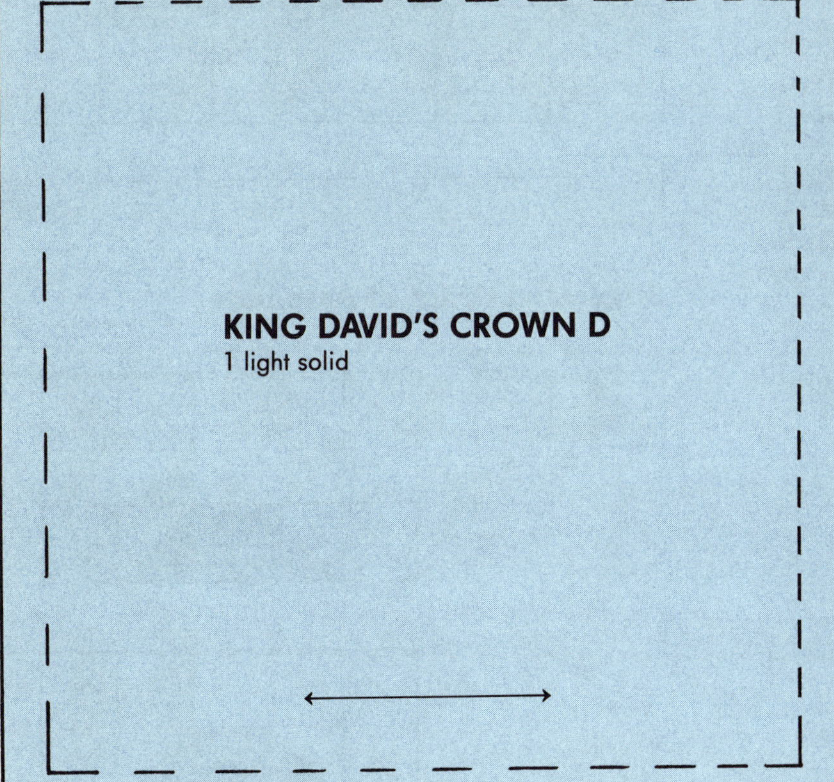

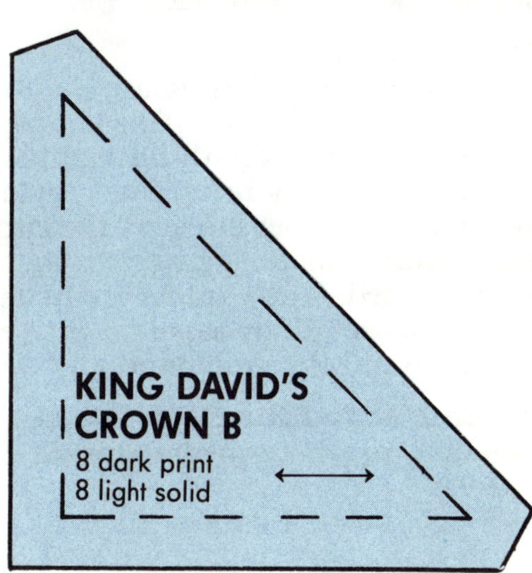

Alternative Project

This pattern would make an attractive small table cover for a side table or for a centerpiece on a banquet table.

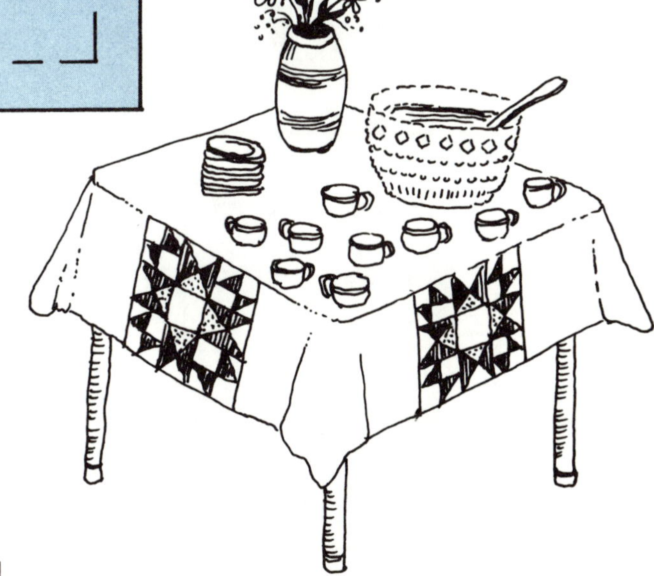

CROWN OF THORNS

Alternative Names
Georgetown Circle, Single Wedding Ring, Crown and Thorns, Old Scraps Patchwork

Variations
This pattern can be done using only light and dark fabrics. The inner circle may be made of two different fabrics.

Bible Verse: John 19:2-3
The soldiers twisted together a crown of thorns and put it on his head. They clothed him in a purple robe and went up to him again and again, saying, "Hail, O king of the Jews!" And they struck him in the face.

Pattern Notes
The triangles with their sharp points make up the thorns of the crown. This simple pattern can be very striking with the right selection of plain and pattern fabrics. The regular combination of a plain inner circle with coordinating print "thorns" against a light background is recommended. Whole quilts are usually made with blocks set off by sashing, with each crown in a different color combination.

Pieces Needed for Each Block
A—4 dark print, 12 medium print, 16 light solid
B—5 light solid, 4 dark print

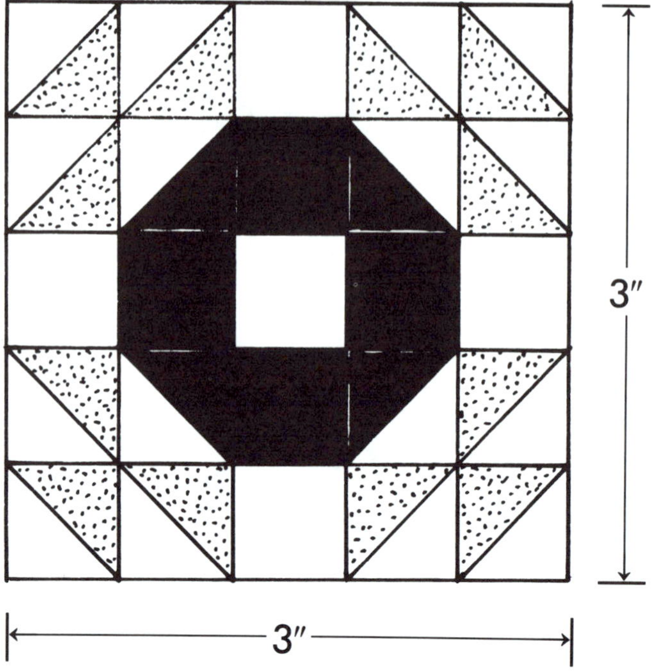

Suggested Order of Assembly

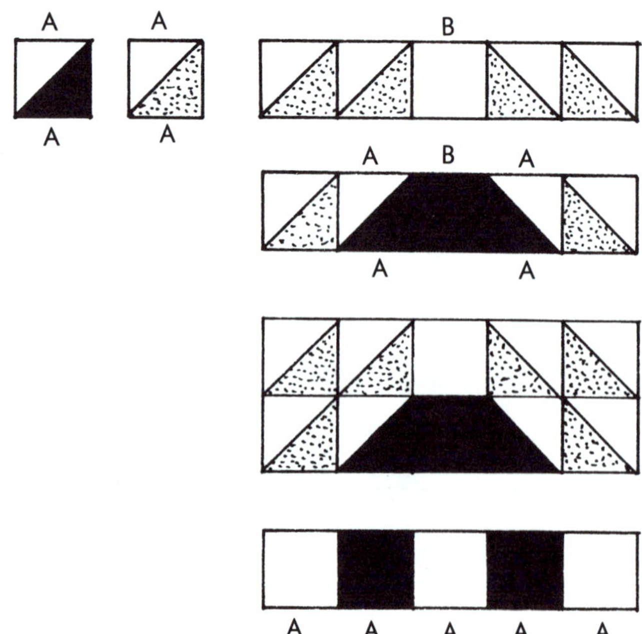

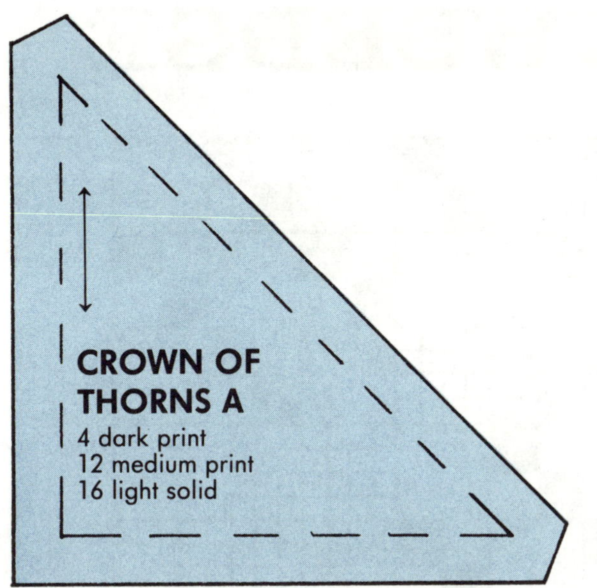

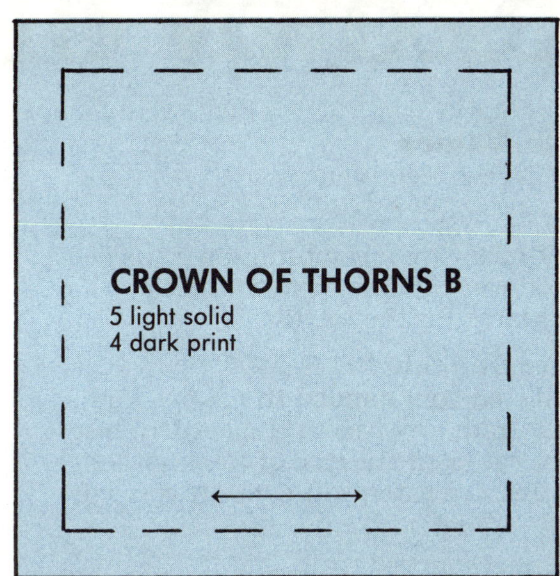

Alternative Project

Design storage bags for communion ware. These can be lined with soft flannel or a napped fabric. Closures can be drawstring or Velcro.

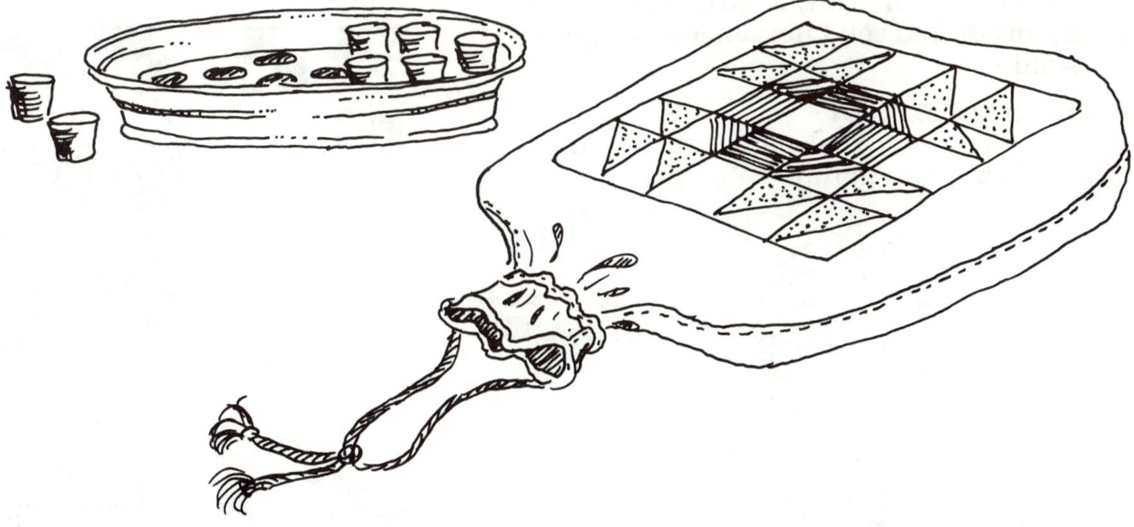

TREE OF KNOWLEDGE

Alternative Names
Tree of Life, Tree of Temptation

Variations
Many tree patterns are a combination of pieced and appliqued work. Some have triangles instead of squares for the leaves.

Bible Verse: Genesis 2:16-17
And the Lord God commanded the man, "You are free to eat from any tree in the garden; but you must not eat from the tree of the knowledge of good and evil, for when you eat of it you will surely die."

Pattern Notes
When done all in green, this pattern makes a lovely tree. The red blocks represent the fruit of the tree. The trunk of the tree is pieced. A complete quilt of this block creates an overall orchard effect.

Pieces Needed for Each Block
A—2 light solid
B—1 dark brown solid
C—1 light solid
D—14 dark green print, 2 dark brown solid
E—22 bright red solid (for apples), 22 light solid

Alternative Project
This pattern would make an attractive and colorful bib for an apron.

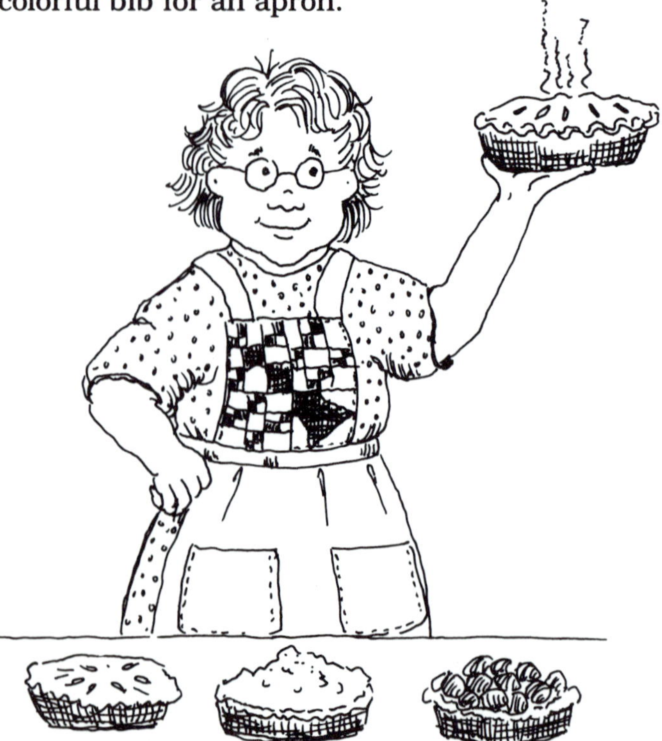

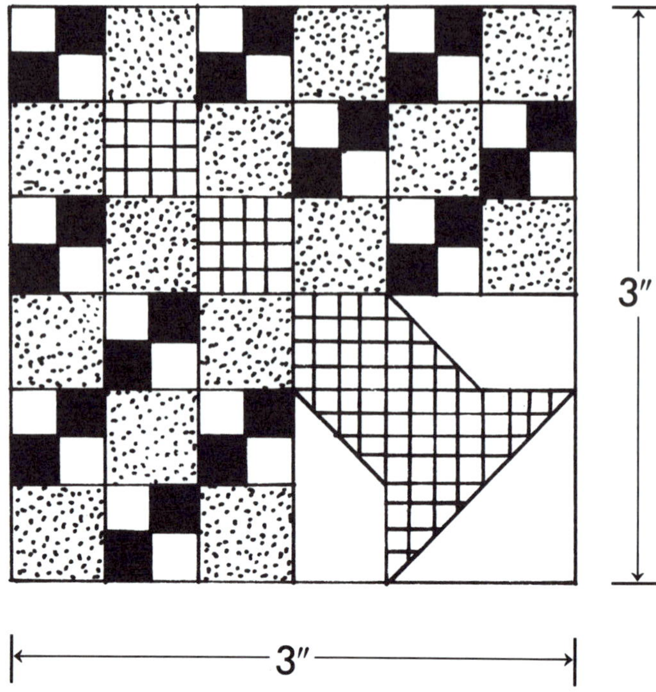

Suggested Order of Assembly

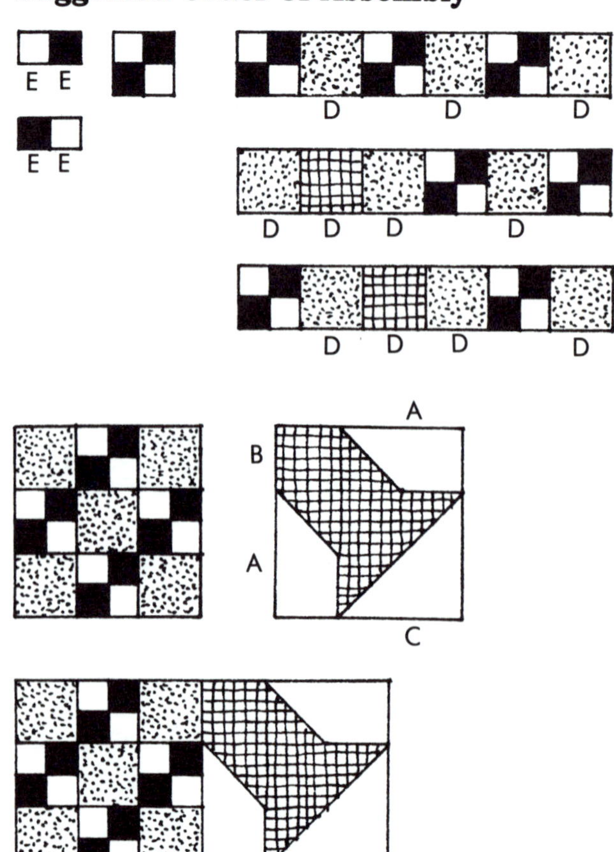

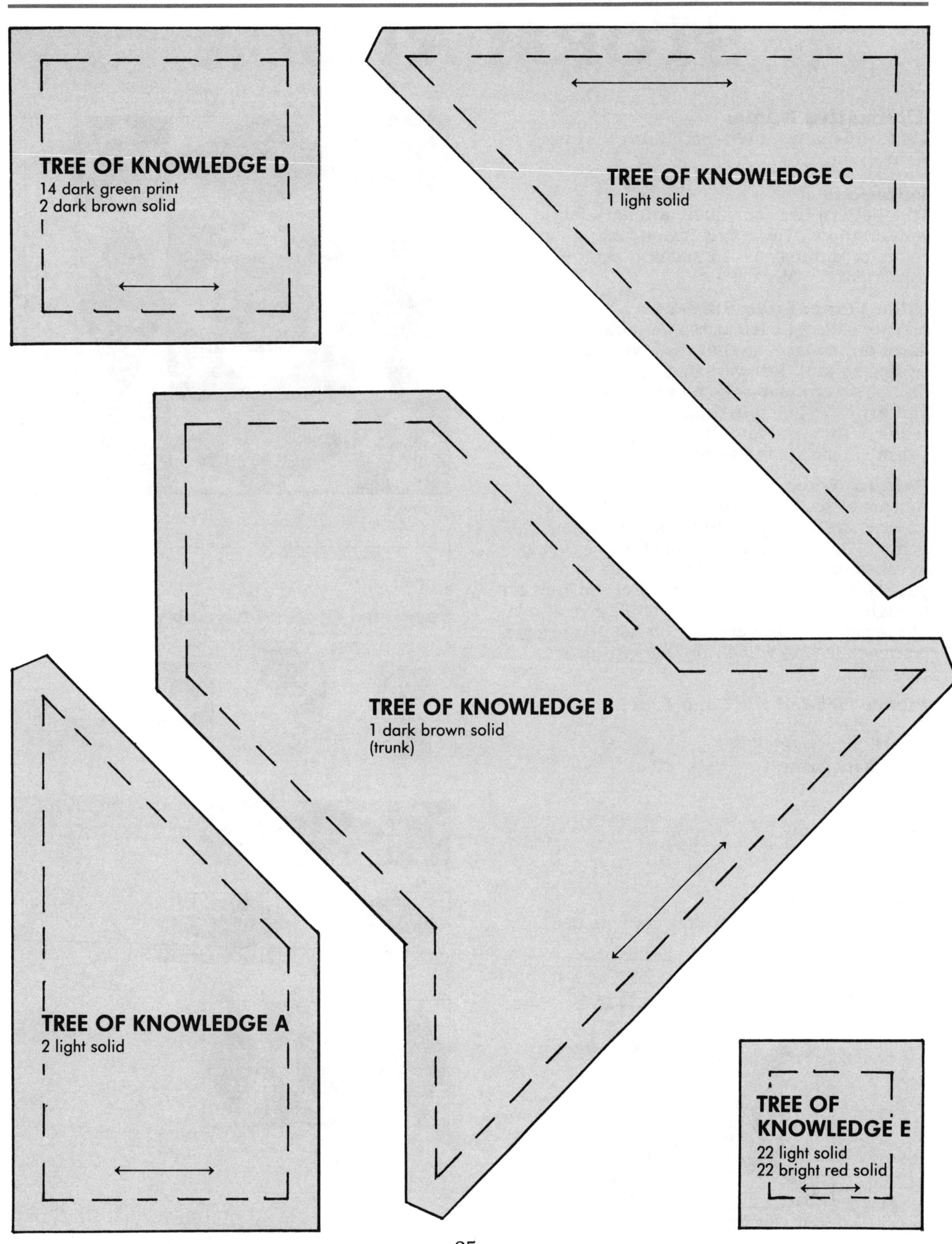
TREE OF KNOWLEDGE D
14 dark green print
2 dark brown solid
TREE OF KNOWLEDGE C
1 light solid
TREE OF KNOWLEDGE B
1 dark brown solid
(trunk)
TREE OF KNOWLEDGE A
2 light solid
TREE OF KNOWLEDGE E
22 light solid
22 bright red solid

STORM AT SEA

Alternative Names
There are many pattern variations that use the same name.

Variations
This pattern uses only light and dark fabric combinations. Variations include using more colors or eliminating the smallest square in the corners of the block.

Bible Verse: Luke 8:23-24
As they sailed, he fell asleep. A squall came down on the lake, so that the boat was being swamped, and they were in great danger. The disciples went and woke him, saying, "Master, Master, we're going to drown!" He got up and rebuked the wind and the raging waters; the storm subsided, and all was calm.

Pattern Notes
Storms at sea must have created terrifying experiences for sailors in the small, fragile boats of Jesus' day. A storm left St. Paul shipwrecked on the island of Malta. This quilt pattern is an optical illusion. All of the lines are straight but the variations in angle give a wave-like sensation. Quilters say they sometimes get a seasick feeling while working with this pattern.

Pieces Needed for Each Block
A—16 dark print
B—16 light solid
C—4 dark print
D—16 light solid
E—4 dark print
F—4 dark print
G—4 light solid
H—1 dark print

Alternative Project
A wall hanging is an attractive way to use this pattern.

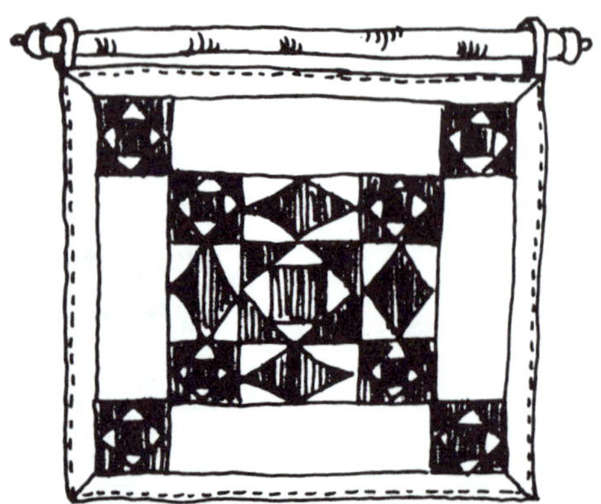

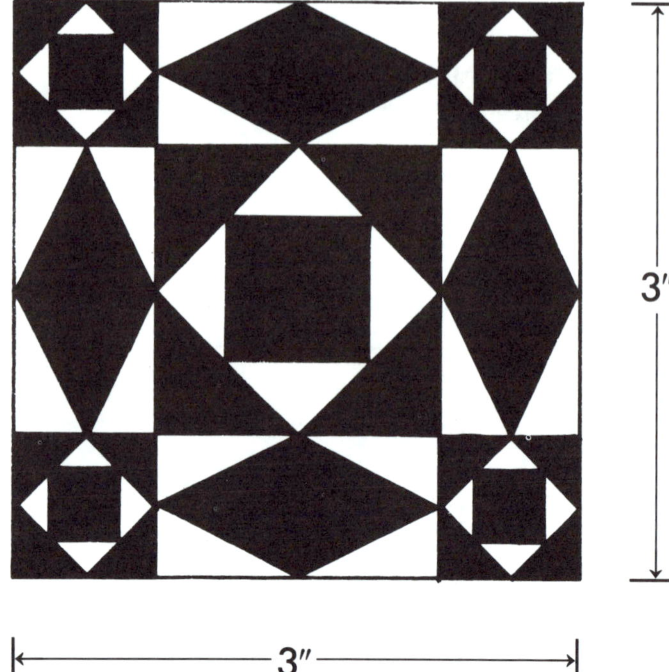

Suggested Order of Assembly

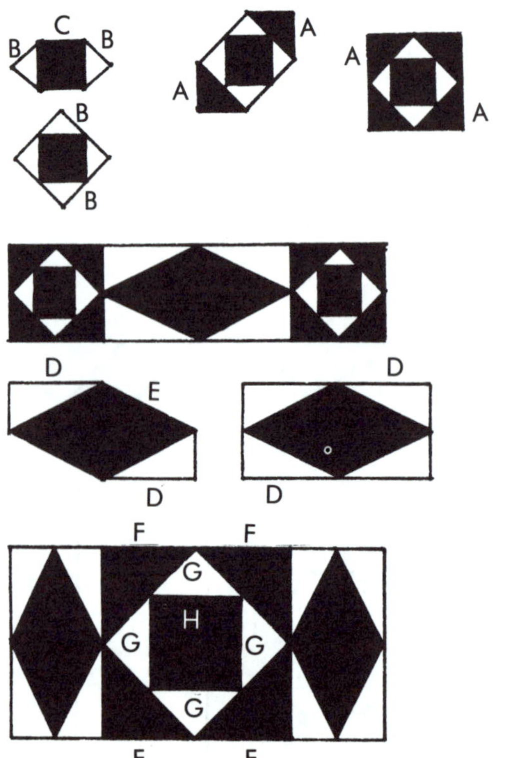

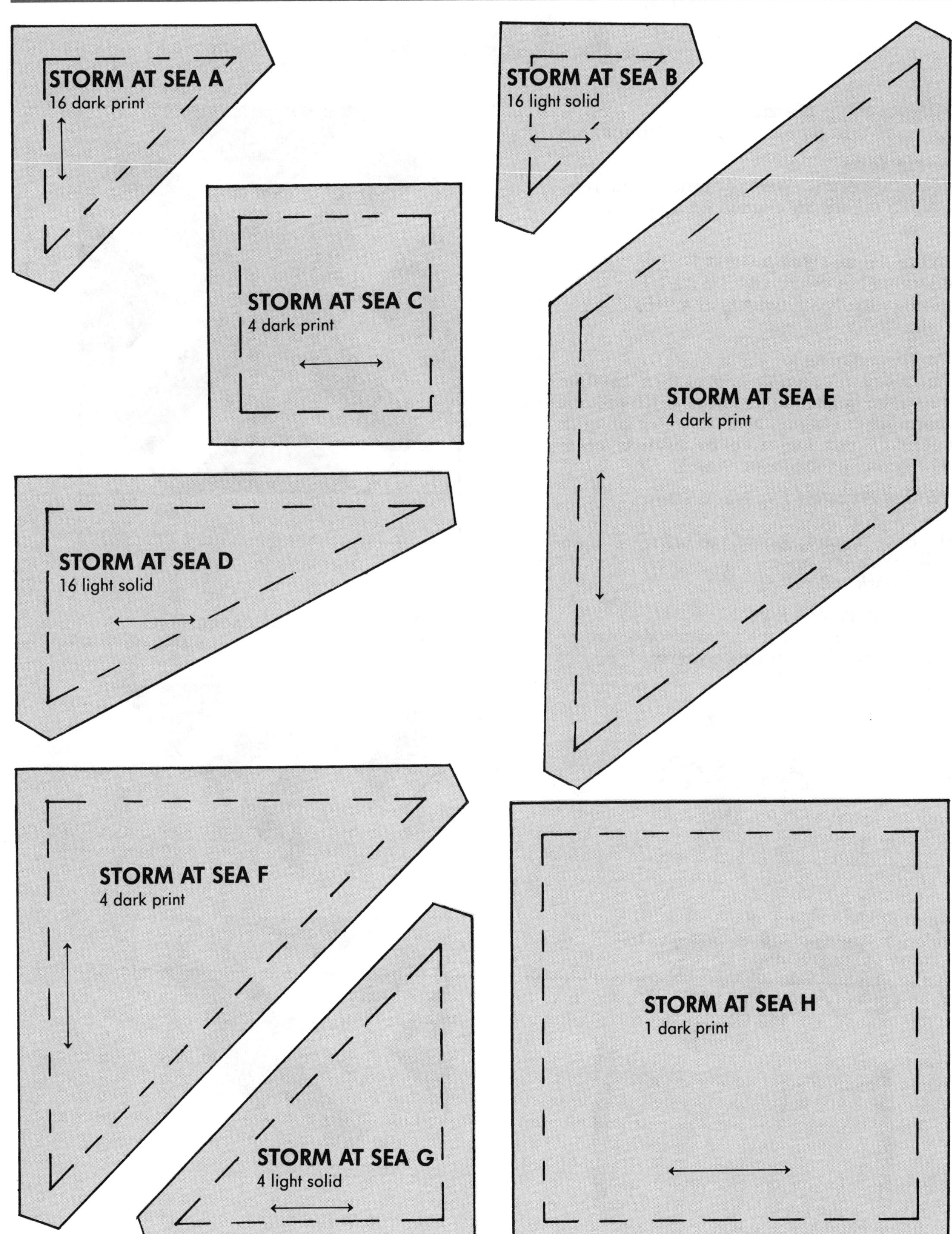
STORM AT SEA A
16 dark print
STORM AT SEA B
16 light solid
STORM AT SEA C
4 dark print
STORM AT SEA E
4 dark print
STORM AT SEA D
16 light solid
STORM AT SEA F
4 dark print
STORM AT SEA H
1 dark print
STORM AT SEA G
4 light solid

CROSS

Alternative Names
Cross Within Squares, Cross Within Cross

Variations
There are many cross patterns. Some refer to Christ; others are named for a country or a person.

Bible Verse: John 19:17
Carrying his own cross, he went out to The Place of the Skull (which in Aramaic is called Golgotha).

Pattern Notes
The most common symbol of the Christian faith, the cross, is used in all art forms and in many sizes, shapes, and details. This quilt pattern is reminiscent of St. Andrew's cross, which was in the form of an X.

Pieces Needed for Each Block
A—4 light solid
B—8 light solid, 4 dark red print
C—4 dark red print
D—1 dark red print

Alternative Project
A small table cover for private communion could be made from this pattern.

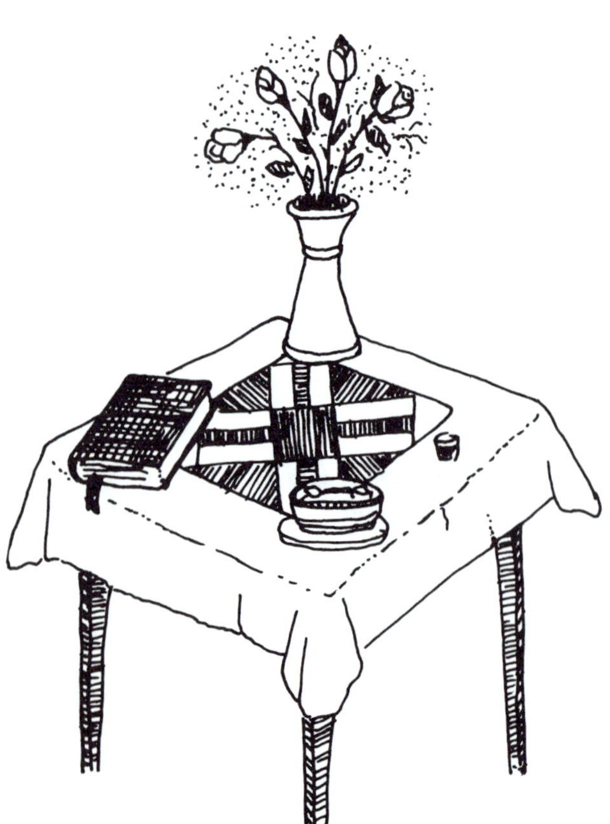

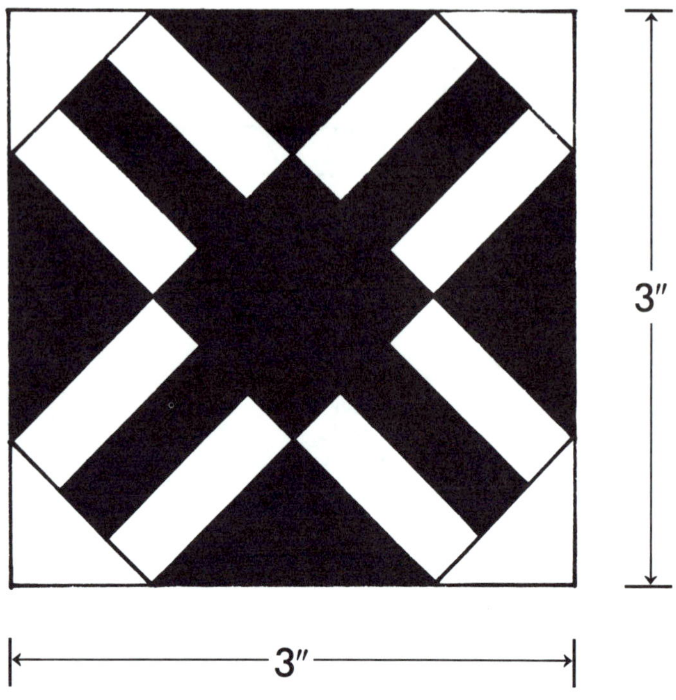

Suggested Order of Assembly

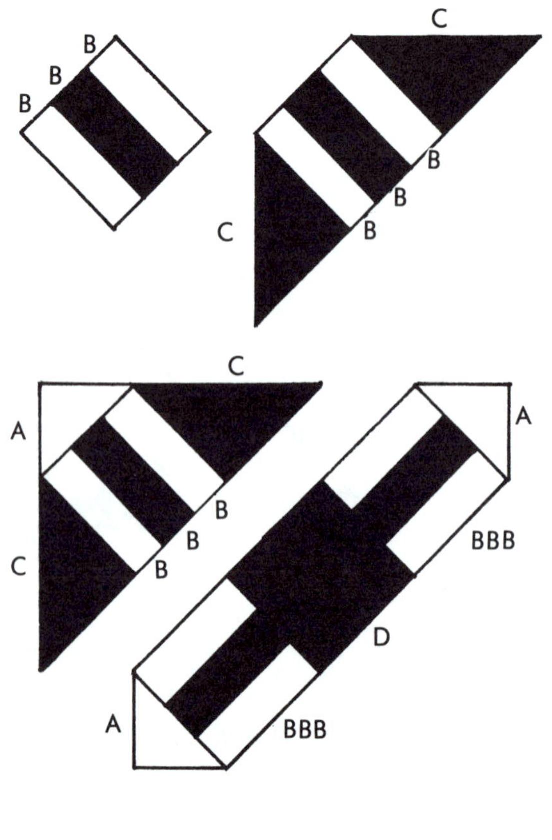

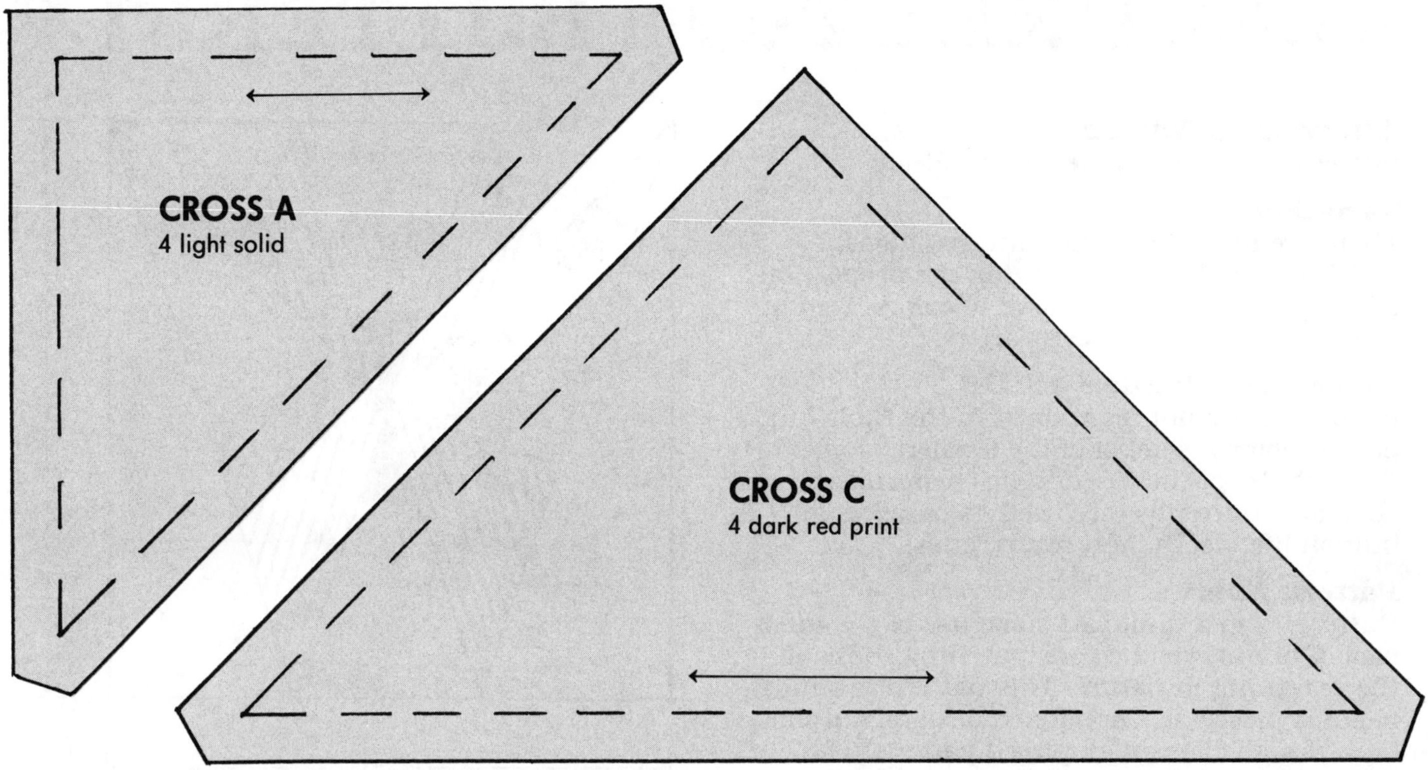

CROSS A
4 light solid

CROSS C
4 dark red print

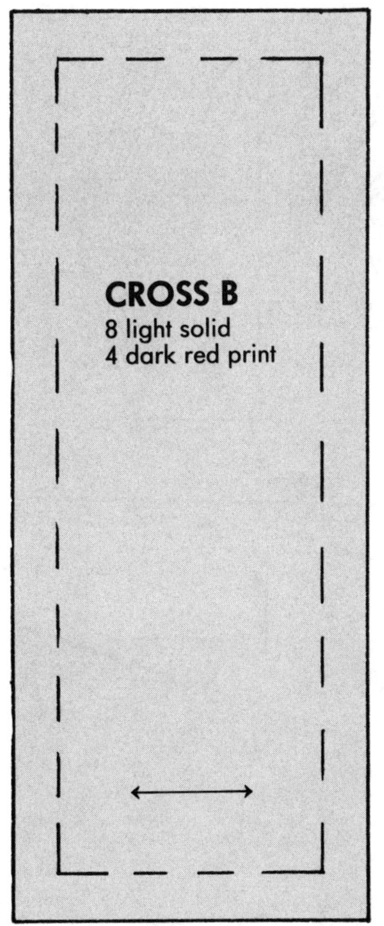

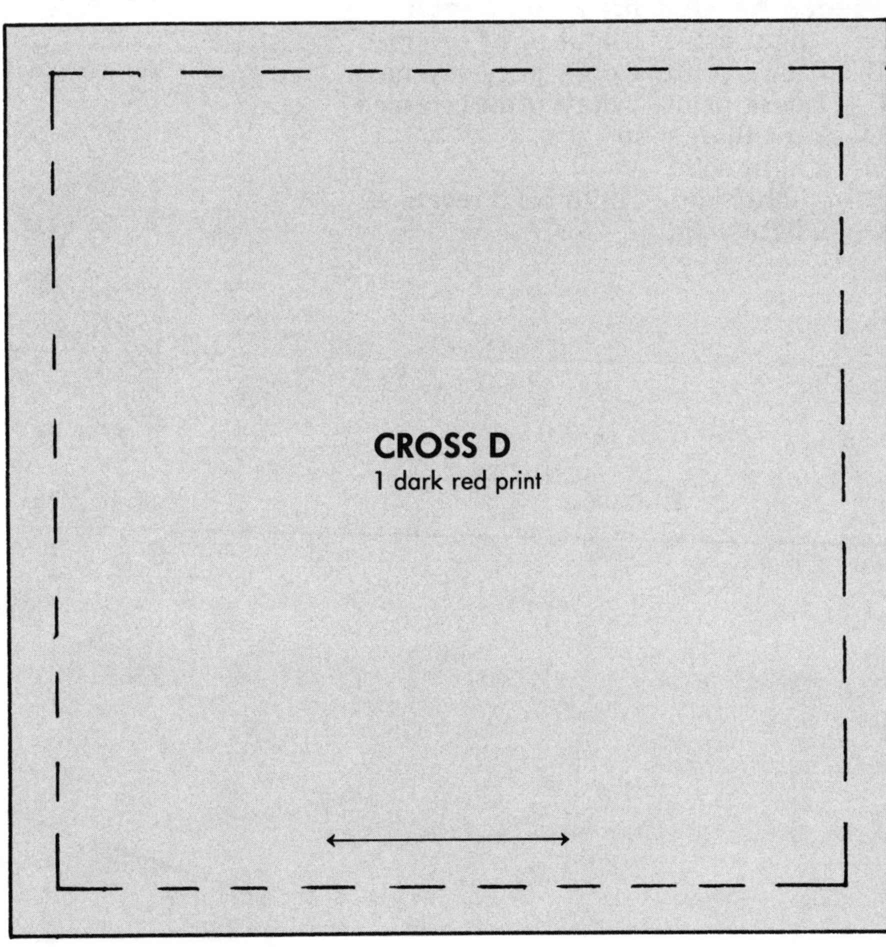

RESURRECTION BUTTERFLY

Alternative Names
Butterflies, Old-fashioned Butterflies

Variations
There are many butterfly patterns, most of which are appliqued. Changing the proportion of the pieces and the number of colors used in this pattern offers endless variety.

Reference: Matthew 28:1-6
Butterflies are not mentioned in the Bible but have become a symbol of the Resurrection. The three stages of the insect's life—caterpillar, chrysalis, butterfly—are used as parallels to human life, death, and resurrection.

Pattern Notes
Butterflies in a quilt can make use of the interplay of bright, vivid colors matching those of the real thing in nature. This pattern is similar to some pieced and appliqued designs but has been designed as an all-pieced pattern. The addition of the antennae gives each butterfly a direction. Almost any combination of bright colors looks good in this pattern.

Pieces Needed for Each Block
A—1 light print, 1 light print reversed
B—1 dark print, 1 dark print reversed
C—1 dark print, 1 dark print reversed
D—2 medium solid
E—2 light solid
F—1 light solid, 1 light solid reversed
G—2 light solid

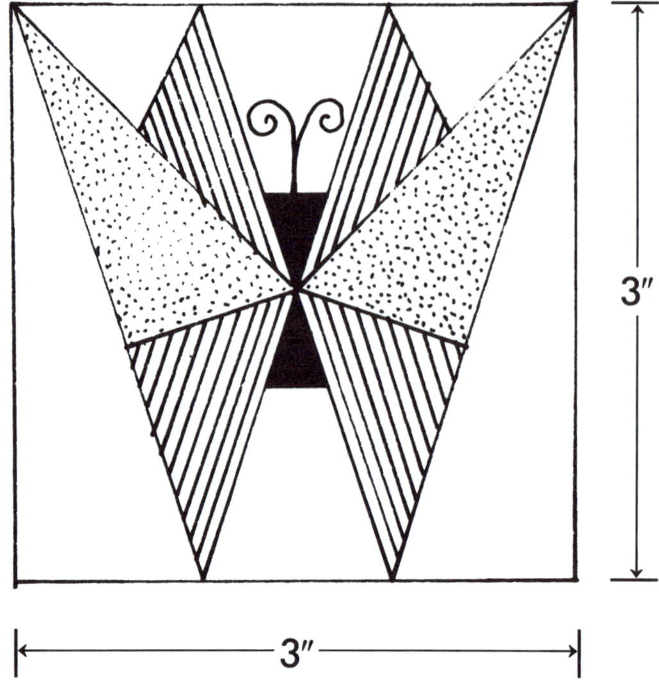

Suggested Order of Assembly

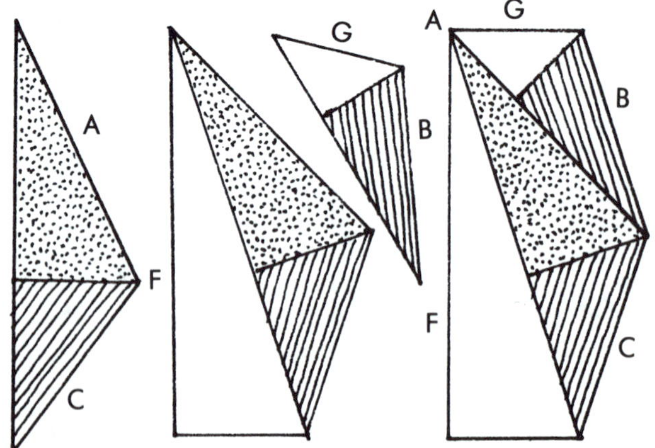

NOTE: Make second piece in reverse

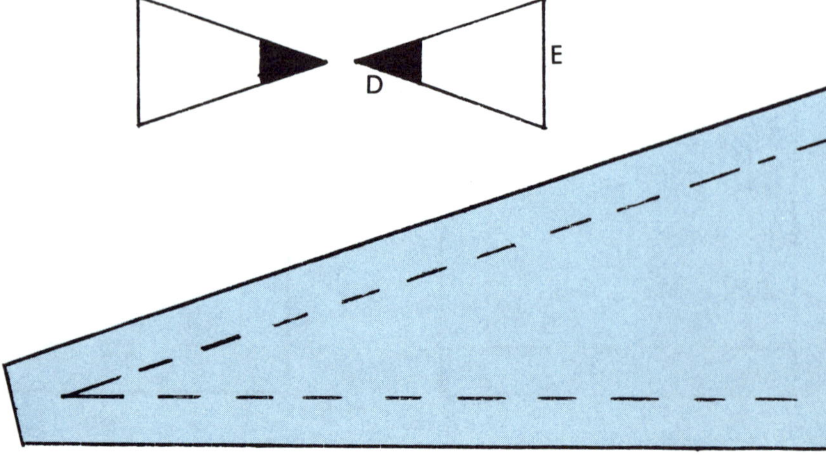

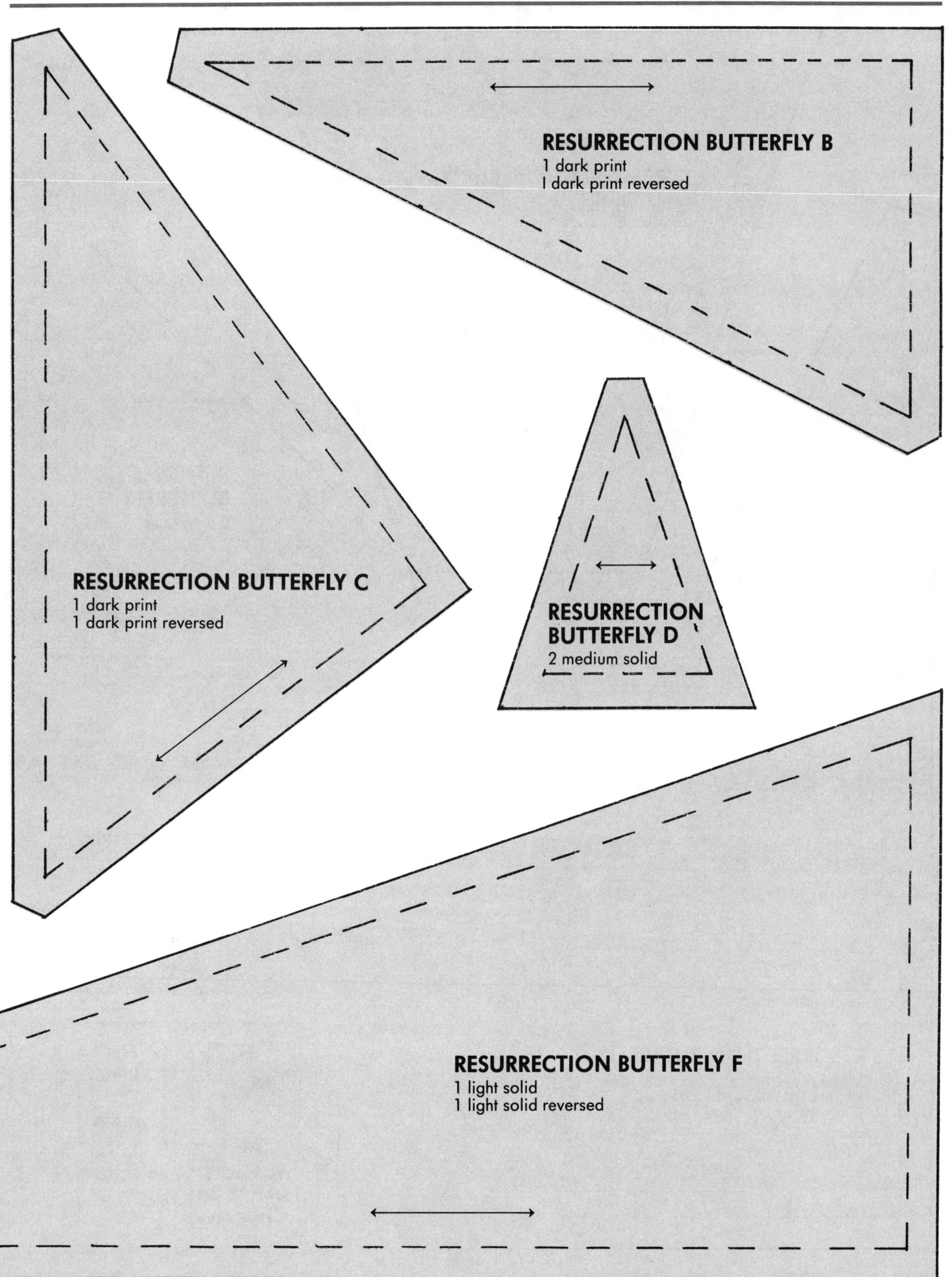
RESURRECTION BUTTERFLY B
1 dark print
I dark print reversed
RESURRECTION BUTTERFLY C
1 dark print
1 dark print reversed
RESURRECTION BUTTERFLY D
2 medium solid
RESURRECTION BUTTERFLY F
1 light solid
1 light solid reversed

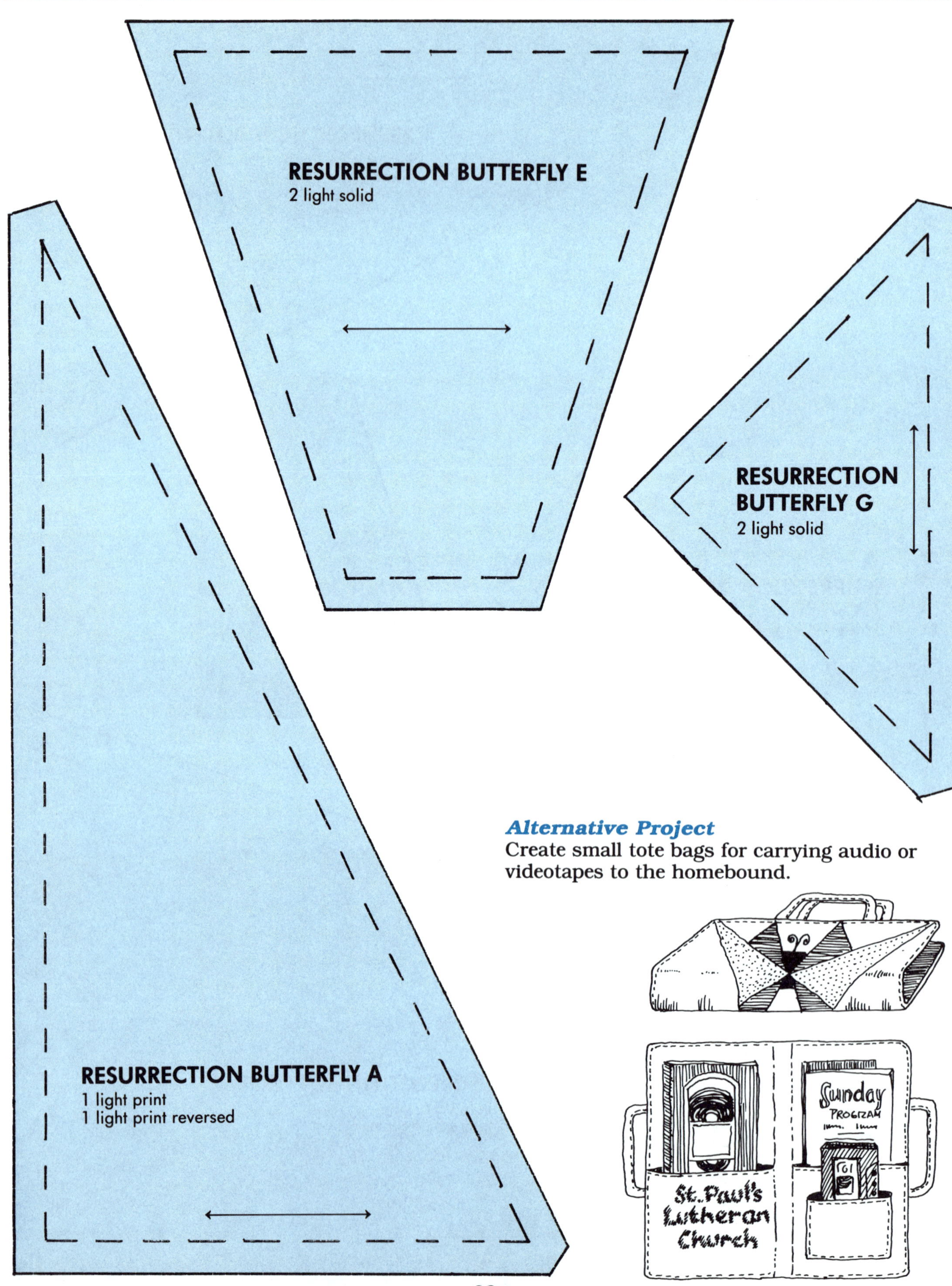

Alternative Project

Create small tote bags for carrying audio or videotapes to the homebound.